Finally Unrestricted

Nova

iUniverse, Inc.

Bloomington

Finally Unrestricted

iUniverse books may be ordered through booksellers or by contacting:

iUniverse
1663 Liberty Drive
Bloomington, IN 47403
www.iuniverse.com
1-800-Authors (1-800-288-4677)

ISBN: 978-1-4502-7942-0 (pbk)
ISBN: 978-1-4502-7943-7 (cloth)
ISBN: 978-1-4502-7944-4 (ebk)

Printed in the United States of America

iUniverse rev. date: 1/25/2011

Finally Unrestricted, a memoir that spans the course of five years, tells a tale of betrayal, redemption, and what it means to have a dream and lose it.

I, Nova, "Nova" Wallace, was born on May 1, 1981, the third of five children. I grew up in the inner city of Lansing, Michigan. No one—especially not my family—-expected me to make much of myself. College was hardly in my family's vocabulary.

Today I am a graduate of Western Michigan University. I hold a bachelor's degree in English/creative writing and an associate's degree from Lansing Community College. I wrote this memoir based on the time I spent studying at Western Michigan University and my personal experience on the Judge Joe Brown show. This story is an actual account of what I went through as a new homeowner, single mother, and college student.

A Thank-You Poem for my Son

Praises to my son for loving me genuine and sincere.
When life turned dark and cold for me, you still loved me,
you still cared,
Even through my triumphs, trials, and tribulations,
Even through the surprises, upheavals, and
graduations.

A fatherless child seemingly destined to be forgotten,
Like your ancestors in the kitchen and in the field
picking cotton,
And just like the slave, you shall rise and succeed
Because you're the newest generation, the strongest
branch on the tree.

You showed courage by being strong during times of war.
Because of you, I survived to be downtrodden nevermore.
This is a thank you, son, for being everything that
I need.
You gave me dignity and pride, replacing my somber
dreams.

I love you, little junior, for all that you've done.
And that is why I wrote this poem especially for you,
my sweet son.

INTRODUCTION

AT FIFTEEN YEARS OLD, I was poverty-level poor and expecting my first child. It was a trying time for me. I had little resources to depend on and no true friends.

I was a high school student at the time, and even though I had my son at a young age, I graduated on time with my class—the class of 1999.

I didn't do much after graduation. I went to work at Lear Corporation, a factory that produced seats for General Motors. And I started my first semester at Lansing Community College.

Then my life took an unexpected turn when I accepted a position as a full-time production assembler with General Motors shortly before my twentieth birthday. That was it. That job was the change my life had been waiting for. It was then that I got off the welfare line.

By the time I was twenty-three, I was who people were talking about—me and my brand new Cadillac CTS, that is. And if they knew me personally, they knew I had just moved into a newly purchased condo on the south side of Lansing, Michigan. That brought on more hate.

It was amusing to me at first. I was the girl who'd started off with nothing, and now I had more than what little my family had refused to share. I now loaned them money. And I was never stingy; I never said no if I knew my family truly needed what they were asking to borrow. I remembered what it felt like to be without.

I had skipped school for no other reason than not having the right clothes. I remembered when my hair was uncombed, and I felt embarrassed to be seen. So I didn't mind helping my little brothers get new clothes or my sisters buy new Coach purses.

I still remember what it felt like to not have pampers for

my baby or money and a ride to the store to buy him any. The numb of the cold as I trekked from the bus stop still haunts my memories like a strong aroma left long after a tart meal.

I turned twenty-four. I didn't know it then, but it was the beginning of the end of the good years for me. A new poverty awaited me. New problems with new issues far more debilitating than the ones I'd managed to escape. Yet there was one thing that remained constant through it all—the people who were causing me trouble.

At twenty-four, I was ready to face my past and myself. I opened my life back up to Grey the father of my eight-year-old son, Jonathan. Grey lived with his girlfriend and was careful not to let her know we had begun seeing each other. Our son wasn't allowed over at his house; nor did Jonathan's dad spend more than a few minutes with him when he came to visit. But that wasn't the point. I was at a place in my life where I felt I needed to know why I wasn't wanted by Grey and why he had left me behind.

I turned twenty-four on May 1, 2005, and on May 11, I graduated from Lansing Community College with my associate's degree in general education. On May 17, I had surgery on my left shoulder as a result of an injury I'd received while working at GM. But my life was just beginning. I had just moved into my condo four months earlier, and I was in celebration mode. The college degree from LCC and the fact that I no longer had to report to work, my doctor had said that I would be unable to work until I healed, opened up new opportunities for my life.I was having fun. It was an exciting time. On the weekends, I went to Detroit to visit with friends. For the first time, I dropped my guard, and I started being me. I wasn't ashamed of myself, even though my family still treated me as if I should be. But I didn't listen to them—that much. I lived my life and tried to be me.

Now my only problem was that my friends and family began to compete with me, and we could no longer have fun together. Going from nothing to seemingly everything had destroyed my closest relationships.

I didn't know it then, but it would only get worse. If having nothing was a huge issue, trying to get something brought on more struggle. I didn't let the hate get me down though. I believed that I had redeemed myself. I understood the choices I'd made by becoming a teenage mother and the people those choices had hurt. But I'd paid my dues. I realized that I didn't owe anybody anything, and so I moved on.

I'd contemplated the idea of leaving Lansing for years. I felt as if I was ready for something else. At first I wanted to move to a major city, maybe New York or LA. Then an opportunity presented itself shortly before my twenty-fifth birthday. I was accepted at Western Michigan University. I'd applied on a whim and unexpectedly I was accepted. I packed only the necessities, sold or gave away the rest, and Jonathan and I left for college.

It was there in Kalamazoo that my life erupted. Every issue, difficulty, crisis, dilemma, hindrance, obstruction, snag, glitch, drawback, or challenge in my life suddenly exploded. I had ignored one problem after another until I was forced to face reality. And for me, that reality was Judge Joe Brown.

What did I learn standing in front of Judge Joe Brown explaining why I was suing my youngest brother? I learned the consequences of playing the fool for far too long. I realized that it was time for me to stop caring about what others had to say about me or my life because trying to please everyone else was the reason I could never be happy.

My biggest error was that I didn't listen to my own voice of reason. I silenced how I felt for the sake of those around me. And it cost me. I'm okay now. I changed my game plan, and I'm going at it from a different direction. I've learned from my mistakes and so have those around me.

So where am I now? I'm at a place no one can get to—a place no earthly being can penetrate. I'm in a world that I've created—a world far away from my haters. Even though I thought it would be impossible, I've left drama behind.

And to my son's father, Grey, there are so many words left

unspoken. In so many ways, I want to tell you and show you what you've done to my life. I want you to see and know how your choices have affected me. But that will never happen. We've moved on. I'm happy, and I know you feel the same. We made the most out of our lives and what little we were given. I've learned not to make enemies. So I hope that, one day, we can evolve and be cordial.

Let me devote a few paragraphs to my family because, without you, I wouldn't be who I am. Your job was to teach me, to show me the meaning of life and who I am. Every member had a specific role and each role a specific purpose in my development. You did your job, and I'm grateful. You didn't kick me out, and I can never repay you for that.

Today my employment, through writing my books, is to go out and give testimony to the things I've learned. My book isn't intended to destroy us. It's to make us better. So after all that, I have to say this: all children grow up, even me.

As a final thought I would like to say this. To those who may feel offended by my book and to the people who think that they are actually a character in my book, I didn't write this book for you. I wrote this book for me and for those who want to learn from my mistakes. I've messed up time and time again; my book is a testimony to that. But after each fall, I rose and overcame. I hope you can do the same.

CHAPTER ONE:
House Party

By FEBRUARY 2005, I had settled into my newly purchased condo. Unpacked and organized, I had a chance to explore life. I enjoyed being a homeowner. It was a much different experience than being a renter. I felt safer in the knowledge that I couldn't be evicted for any apparent reason, and I had a deep sense of accomplishment.

I was different now—high-class, at least in my own mind. My future looked better than I'd possibly imagined.

I was usually depressed, but in my condo, I felt like a different person. I got dressed up every day. I went to the hair salon every two weeks. I put on makeup most days. I wore high heels.

Yet, I had nowhere to go. Lansing, Michigan, was a small city.

To amuse myself, I sometimes drove down Martin Luther King Boulevard, trying to see who was out. I drove past M9's party store, once a popular hangout for teenagers. The only customers there now were for Metro Music and Paging located next door.

Tired of driving around in a circle, I spent the majority of my time in the condo with my seven-year-old son, Jonathan. Jonathan and I hung out together. We went to the movies and out to eat at our favorite restaurants often. Sometimes we even played video games together, but I was still somewhat lonely. I wanted the company of adult friends.

My youngest brother, Green, came to live with me in the condo, although he never officially moved in and he was gone most of the time so he didn't count as a friend.

Tired of being bored, I decided to throw card parties at my house and invite a few of my friends. My first card party took place in March 2005.

I was twenty-three years old at the time, and so was Alyson, a high school friend of mine. Topaz, a girl I'd met while working at my high school job, was a year behind us. They were excited when I told them about the card party I wanted to have. I even provided the men. I got the hookup on the guys from my son's barber.

I took Jonathan to Constellation's Barber Shop located in the Logan Square on the south side. Constellation's was one of the most popular barber shops in Lansing. People came not only to get their hair cut, but to show off the latest fashions as well.

Danny was my son's regular barber. He was tall, slim figured, and had a chestnut complexion. He stayed clean shaven and neat. He was decent-looking but not my type.

"My manz Q's been asking about you," Danny said one day in early March when I brought Jonathan in to get his hair cut.

That sparked my interest. I'd been doing nothing for weeks. I was bored and wanted entertainment.

"For real? What he say?" I asked.

"He said that you're cute. He wanted to know if you had a man."

I tried to get another look at Q. He worked three stations down from Danny. Q's most noticeable feature was his square jaw. Like his jawline, his forehead was a perfect square. Even the back of his head was shaped like a square. His small nose was a small square, and his lips were nothing more than an elongated square when closed. We were nearly the exact same honey brown complexion. Q had potential.

"Does he have a girl?" I asked.

"He said he was single. Give me your number, and I'll give it to him."

I was hesitant. I scarcely dated around town because Lansing was so small. I decided to take a chance. After all, I had nothing to lose. I was single and interested in dating. I wrote my number down on a piece of paper and handed it to Danny before I left.

My first date with Q was the card party I threw at my house.

Q said he had a few friends to bring. I called up Alyson and Topaz, and we made plans for that Friday night.

The first card party was fun. Q came over with six of his friends. They brought liquor and a pack of playing cards. Topaz brought her white friend, Kristina. Alyson came alone.

For once, I wasn't bored on a Friday night. I learned how to make my own fun, and we had a good time drinking, playing cards, and listening to music. Most importantly, I had something exciting to talk about throughout the week. I was showing everyone that you could have it all.

We decided to do it again the following weekend with the same people. This time my cousin, Gabby, would be coming along. Gabby had just turned twenty and wanted to hang out.

Gabby didn't have a car, and neither did Alyson. So I picked them up in my new ride. Two days earlier, I'd turned in the lease to my 2001 Ford Explorer and leased a 2005 Cadillac CTS.

I loved my Cadillac. It was gray and a base model, but it was a Cadillac.

I picked Gabby up first and made the quick drive toward the mall to where Alyson stayed.

"Did you tell Topaz about your feelings for James?" Alyson asked me while we were driving back to my house.

I took a deep breath and continued driving. *I'ma have to cut her off again. I see now that she's still on the same shit. The bitch ain't changed since high school. You shouldn't have told her you still liked James. She's just mad it ain't her.*

I gave Alyson a slighted smile and said in a lighthearted tone, "No, because I think it's nothing more than a crush. Sometimes you just have crushes on people. I've learned to just get over it."

I made eye contact with Alyson in the rearview mirror. I gave her an evil look. She turned away. I knew then that my friendship with Alyson was ending for good. We'd had problems since high school, and I was tired of it. Regardless of how Alyson felt about me having a crush on Topaz's man, she was my friend, and that was our secret. She didn't even know Topaz.

"Your car is fresh," Gabby said to me.

"Thanks. I just got it."

Gabby ran her hands over the dashboard. "Nice," she said.

Alyson remained silent in the back seat.

Topaz, Kristina, Alyson, Gabby, and I had some time to hang out together before Q and his friends arrived. I knew all of the girls separately, but as a group, we were strangers.

We sat in my living room talking and trying to get a feel for each other. I had private conversations with all the girls, and they told me that they wanted to hang out with a group. We had all watched *Sex in the City*. We were young, single women. We wanted to be just like the TV girls. I brought them all together to give it a try.

"I plan on going to school in the fall. I'm young and don't have any kids, so I feel that right now I can do anything," Gabby said.

Gabby sat to the right of me. I had pulled a chair from the dining room and sat facing the rest of the girls. We sat in a semicircle. I was relaxed and watchful. I didn't trust Alyson around Topaz. I could tell that Alyson was jealous of my life. I got the feeling that she would try and ruin my friendship with Topaz if she got the chance.

"That's good that you don't have any kids," I said to Gabby.

"I know. I love not having any kids," she said.

I knew what Gabby was doing. Topaz and Kristina both had no children. I only had one, but Alyson had two children by two different men, and she had a complex about it. Still pissed about Alyson asking about James, I let Gabby dig.

Not only was Alyson the only girl there with two children, she was also the darkest and the fattest. She was cute, but she had low self-esteem about her look. She wore her hair pulled up with a crinkly drawstring ponytail attached. Her edges looked hard and gelled. She had a large stomach, a flat behind, and dark spots on her hands and arms.

Gabby's complexion was medium brown, light-skinned

according to Alyson's standards. She had a small waist and a large behind that she shamelessly flaunted in a pair of tight pants.

"That's so good you don't have any kids. You can do anything when you don't got any kids," I said.

"Ain't that right," Topaz chimed in, and we let out a chuckle.

Alyson remained quiet.

Topaz was pretty. She had long, silky hair and stood about five foot seven. She had smooth, almond skin. Her mother was half white. That's where she got her "mixed" look from.

Topaz was naturally quiet and watchful. Sometimes she could be a loud and mean person, but mostly, she kept to herself. Sometimes she was shy and awkward, and at other times she was bullish and straightforward. I loved her personality. Topaz was a Taurus like Alyson and me. Our birthdays were only days apart.

I glanced over at Kristina. Kristina was abnormally pale. She wore her strawberry blonde hair slicked back into a long ponytail. She was frail and awkwardly built. I hated her and only tolerated her because she was Topaz's best friend. I felt that Kristina had a jealous heart and felt inadequate around pretty black women, especially me.

Kristina sat quietly and listened. She never said a word and never joined in our conversation. The vibe I got from her was that she was there to watch Topaz's back. It was understandable. When black women got together, usually there was drama.

Alyson, feeling trapped, switched the conversation and began talking about marriage. That led to her discussing her parent's marriage. "My dad is such a good father and husband," she said. "Sometimes when I've given up on finding a good man, I think about my dad and what a good man he is, and I know that there are good men still out there."

The look on Topaz's face was blank. I turned to get a look at Gabby. She seemed worried and nervous. I knew Gabby had a complex about her dad. He hadn't been around much when she was growing up.

I knew that both Topaz and Kristina came from dysfunctional families. They were silent. So was I. Alyson was aware of the issues between my dad and me. We had been friends since I was fifteen. She had seen a lot.

Alyson had a slight smirk on her face, as if she had cornered us. I looked at Alyson and with a bland expression on my face said, "Yeah."

Silence followed. Alyson's parents were the last thing we wanted to talk about.

The conversation moved on. Alyson didn't get the gratification she was looking for, so she gave up.

Q and his friends arrived sometime after ten. I watched as the other girls had fun. Topaz and Kristina sat together talking to a couple of guys. Gabby mingled with a guy, and Alyson and I sat at the dining room table playing spades. We were partners. I was glad that she was a strong partner. We won most hands.

The guys danced and joked with each other. They were getting drunk and having a good time. The most interesting of the men was the one they called Uncle. He was big, exceptionally dark, and overweight. He had a missing front tooth and always talked about how broke he was. The other guys gave him money for liquor and cracked jokes on him.

Uncle was loud, and he acted gay even though his friends said he was straight. He was about fifteen years older than Q and his friends. Uncle had come to the first card party, and I was glad he came to the second. He was the entertainment. When I put on music, he got up and danced. However, when he nearly spilled his drink on my living room carpet, the dancing stopped.

Although the card party was fun, there was no time for Q and me to mingle. He sat in one half of the condo, and I entertained in the other. I didn't mind. Then I noticed that Q seemed more interested in talking to Topaz than me. I saw him pull on Topaz's arm. I gave him a look, and he stopped. But it was over from that moment on.

One of Q's friends had brought some weed, and so I busied

myself with trying to get high with Alyson. It turned out that the weed was a fake, and I had to spend the rest of the party playing cards pissed about the fake weed.

The card party ended around three in the morning. I went to bed tired. I awoke the next morning to a knock on my door.

"Yes," I said, answering the door.

"I think this is yours," said a white man as he handed me a Heineken bottle.

I took the bottle in silence. It was from Q and his friends. I was embarrassed.

It had taken Q and his friends some time to leave the parking lot. I had to go outside and tell them to leave. I knew that they were loud, and I worried that they might upset my neighbors. But to leave a bottle in the parking lot was obvious disrespect.

I decided that I would have no more card parties; besides, everyone at my party, with the exception of Gabby, had his or her own apartment. If they wanted to continue the card parties, they'd have to find another venue.

As I knew it would happen, Alyson and I soon officially stopped hanging out. This was a result of what I would take to calling the Q incident.

The Q incident happened the week following the second (and last) card party. Q decided that we needed a private date to get to know each other. It just so happened that Alyson had hooked up with Damar, a friend of Q's who also happened to be a distant cousin of mine.

We decided to meet up at Alyson's house. Q and Damar left us waiting over an hour for our date. I didn't mind because it had been years since I was last in Alyson's townhouse. Alyson and I only periodically kept in contact. In January, she had gotten my number from my mom and called me. I had only been back in her life for a few months.

Alyson and I had stopped hanging out after high school. We had a falling out during our senior year, and we were never the same after that. After high school, I'd taken a job at Lear and later had accepted a position at GM. I had no time for friends especially Allsion. I had Jonathan to take care of all by myself; and besides, Alyson was on welfare. We had nothing in common.

My eyes wondered around as my mind drifted back through time. As I sat in Allyson's living room I came to realize how far we had drifted apart, or perhaps we were never close to begin with.

I stared at Allyson silent and in deep thought. It was then that I understood that I was gazing into the eyes of a stranger.

"I'm fixing the place up," Alyson said, interrupting my thoughts. "I'm getting new furniture when I get my income tax check. Allan has been helping me with Danashia. Derrick still doesn't help with Krisha."

At one point in time, we would have talked about my baby daddy and how I felt about being a single mom. Now there was nothing to say about baby daddies. I hadn't dealt with Grey in years. I had no new stories to tell.

I thought about high school when Alyson was my best friend. Back then, we had been just alike—even though her parents helped her out and so she'd had a lot more than me.

Her parents were good people. They even helped me. Because of the help they gave me in high school, I was able to finish and graduate on time. I'd always acknowledged them as part of the reason I would be graduating from Lansing Community College in May.

When everyone, including my family, had turned their backs on me, the Blue family had been there. When I was in eleventh grade, I'd had to drop out of school temporarily because I had no babysitter.

* * *

Because I was on my dad's insurance, he claimed me on his taxes so in order to determine whether to offer assistance the state looked at his GM income. That meant I didn't qualify for any assistance. Without daycare assistance, I couldn't afford daycare.

My grandma had offered to watch my baby for twenty-five dollars a week, but Dad wouldn't pay. And I had no income.

When Alyson found out why I wasn't going to school, she told her mom. Mrs. Blue called me. I spoke with Mrs. Blue over the phone. She offered to babysit for free while I went to school. "Just pay me whenever you can," she said.

But I still wasn't going to school. I had no transportation back and forth to the Blues' house so I still was unable to attend school. When Alyson found out why I still wasn't in school, she told her mom. Mrs. Blue once again stepped in and helped. Mrs. Blue picked Jonathan up from me on Monday and brought him back to me on Friday. It was a great help to me, but the truth always remains, if a favor appears to be without fault it's usually guilty of something. And soon I came to realize the Blues' dark side. And they're babysitting for me quickly came to an end when Alyson made a joking threat close to the end of the first semester of my junior year of high school. "I'm gonna drop your baby," she said to me, laughing.

"What!" I looked at her in shock. A couple of girls who were standing around us did the same.

"I'm just kidding."

Alyson tried to convince me she was joking for the rest of the day. I didn't believe her. When I got home from school, I told my older sister Asia what she had said.

"That bitch aint playing. She's gonna throw your baby down. Go get him right now," Asia said.

Frustrated, I responded, "I don't have a car. How am I supposed to go and pick him up?"

And for the first time since I had my son, Asia did something nice for me. She gave me a ride over to the Blues' house. I picked Jonathan up after school that day. That was December 1997.

My Aunt Janet watched Jonathan the second semester of junior year for twenty-five dollars a week.

In December 1997, the state of Michigan started paying for my daycare services. I even got back pay. So it worked out that I could afford daycare. I made fifty dollars a week babysitting; plus I made money on the side doing hair.

It had been hard paying Aunt Janet half my income every week, but I'd made it.

* * *

I continued to look around Alyson's apartment. "It looks nice in here. I like your furniture," I said.

Alyson had a velvet sofa set with a black pattern and black, glass tables. It was chic and modern in taste.

Alyson and I laughed and caught up on our lives. I talked about the struggles I faced as a single mom. I told Alyson my feelings.

"You think it's hard," she said. "Try being a single mom with two kids by two different men. The men out here are brutal. It's so hard to explain to people about my two baby daddies. I can't stand Allen now. I feel like he did this to me on purpose. He promised me that he would marry me."

I shook my head, yet I didn't feel sorry for Alyson. I had told her not to have any more children after Danashia was born, especially by Allen. I still couldn't forget the slapping incident.

* * *

"You won't believe what just happened." Alyson had called to tell me.

I was nineteen at the time and still living in Waverly Park, a large apartment complex up the street from where Alyson lived.

"What?" I asked.

"Allen was over here. And Derrick called. He was like, that bitch ass nigga betta' not be there when I get there. I'm on my way. Allen got so scared he wanted to leave. But he couldn't get in his car because it was cold out and his locks were frozen. So he got some hot water and was trying to unfreeze his locks. He was so damn scared. He was shaking and saying, 'Come on, Alyson, bring me some more hot water.' He was in such a hurry trying to get outta there before Derrick came."

We laughed hard.

"Oh, hell no," I said.

"Wait that ain't it. Then Derrick pulled up. He was like, I told yo' bitch ass to be gone by the time I got here. Then he slapped Allen hard in the face. I was standing in the door, and they were in the parking lot, and I could hear it.

Alyson paused and let out a sigh. "Allen started crying," she said.

"Crying?" I asked, shocked and unable to believe it. "No, girl. Please tell me he wasn't crying."

"Yes, girl. A tear rolled down his face. And this is the worst part … he sniffled."

A loud roar of a laugh erupted from me. I laughed so hard I had to put the phone down. "I'm sorry," I said, picking the phone back up. "He sniffled?"

"Yes. Now it was cold outside, and so it could have been from the cold. But he did sniffle."

"Get rid of him. You can't have a man who's that weak. He ain't got no backbone."

"I was thinking the same thing," she said.

But she didn't listen. She went on to have a baby with Allen, and now his revenge was to torture her.

* * *

I felt sorry for Alyson. I knew Allen would dog her out. A weak man can never be trusted. Alyson was the best thing going for Allen, but he was so bent on getting Derrick back for the slap that he purposely dogged her out.

"Fuck Allen," I said. "You can do better. Get you a new man and move on."

We continued sitting in the living room talking. After an hour, I realized the time. I was mad that Q had made me wait so long. "Call them and tell them I left. Don't no man leave me waiting all night," I said, getting up to leave.

"You sure?"

"Yeah, I'm tired," I said. I left and went home.

Alyson called me the next day to tell me about her date with Damar and Q. Since I wasn't there, she had called Sharron, an old cosmetology friend.

"You said you didn't want him, so I called Sharron," Alyson said. "They ended up hooking up. Sharron ended up having sex with him that night."

Let me get this straight, I thought. *I said I didn't want Q, so you called Sharron without asking me first. Sharron comes over and has sex with Q, and now they kick it and you calling to tell me. Okay, fine.*

I paused for a moment, "Wow," I said.

"I know. I called you to tell you because I didn't want to seem fake."

"Oh no, no problem. I said I didn't want him. Besides he looks better with Sharron. I wouldn't have sex with him on the first date, so he went with someone that would."

Alyson had told me before that she had started having sex with Damar shortly after they met during the first card party. The way I saw it, Alyson and Sharron were a tag team.

I saw Alyson a few times after that. I invited her and Topaz over for dinner. We chitchatted and kept it casual, but our friendship was dead. I couldn't trust her at all. She kept up too much drama and had too many sneaky ways. Eventually, we fell out of contact.

*   *   *

I also had problems with my friendship with Topaz. Three weeks after my last card party, Topaz called me and invited me over to her house.

I'd known Topaz for seven years and was still unsure as to

who she was and where our friendship stood. It was time for us to start to spend quality time together as friends.

Then her cell phone began to ring.

"Your phone's ringing," I yelled to Topaz, who was fixing her makeup in the bathroom.

"Who is it?" she asked.

"James."

"Answer it."

I talked with James for a moment. He was brief and to the point.

"James said he's coming over," I said.

My voice didn't sound confident, and I was somewhat nervous. I wanted to make sure I was gone before he got there.

James arrived with a friend shortly after I hung up the phone. The two boys walked in. I couldn't help but notice how good James looked. He had not changed over the years. His eyes were still a warm shade of hazel brown, almost gray. I noticed his flat stomach through his shirt.

I bet he still has a six-pack, I thought.

James sat down on the sofa next to the couch I was sitting on. His friend sat down on the couch with me.

"I know Nova," James said, looking over at me. "I've been knowing Nova for a long time. We go way back." Then he turned to Topaz and gave her an irritated look. "I'm surprised you're not drunk yet," he said.

Topaz laughed his comment off, but she looked uncomfortable. "I haven't started," she said.

I knew right then that there was a serious problem. I thought his comment was mean and embarrassing.

He's on some bullshit. Just play it cool. If it gets too out of hand, leave, I told myself. I continued to watch TV.

"Yeah, me and Nova go way back. We've been friends for a long time," James said.

I couldn't pretend with James. We knew each other very well.

I was uncomfortable and felt cornered. I turned to him and said, "How you doin' James?"

James was once the godfather of my son. He was the one I called when I needed diapers, a ride, money, information about Grey, or a friend to talk to. James was one of my oldest friends, yet there was also a deep sexual attraction between the two of us. And it took extreme restraint not to have sex with him. There was always a reason why James didn't end up with me. In the beginning, it was my shyness.

*　*　*

James had invited me to hang out with him once. It was the end of my freshman year at Sexton.

"Hey, Nova," he said to me as he looked out the second-floor window of J.W. Sexton.

I was feeling great that day. I had survived the ninth grade. I had been violated, sabotaged, scandalized, cast out, preyed upon, silenced, beaten, jumped, humiliated, harassed, and victimized—all of that just to make it to the tenth grade. But I had done it. I was feeling great because it was the last day of school.

I looked up. I was delighted to see James's face smiling down at me. He stopped me and sparked up conversation. I could barely think of words to say. James was the most sought after boy in the ninth and tenth grade.

During the school year, I'd overheard whispers and talk about James. All the girls noticed him. He was sexy and confident. But only the "it" girls got to date him. He was part of the in circle. By the end of the school year, his popularity had reached that of the senior level.

"Whatcha doin'?" he asked.

"On my way home," I said. My eyes stayed fixed on him. "I have a job interview," I added.

"Where at?"

"The movie theatre."

"We're hiring at my job too."

"Where you work?" I asked, trying to sound casual.

I was excited. I knew that he was interested if he was making small talk.

"McDonald's."

"Which one?"

"The one on Saginaw."

"I'ma come up there and fill out an application," I said, walking away.

I didn't want to embarrass myself. I wasn't dressed nicely. I had on an old pair of shorts that were too small and too tight and a faded T-shirt. My shoes were old and worn, and my hair was pulled back into a natural, nappy ponytail. I needed a relaxer.

"You need a ride?" he called out after me.

I stopped walking. "No, my dad will take me."

"I work on the weekends," he said.

"Okay. How old do you have to be to work there?"

"Sixteen."

I was disappointed. I shook my head. "I can't work there. I'm only fifteen."

"When you turn sixteen?"

"Next year, I just turned fifteen."

"They might give you a job. Come fill out an application anyway."

"Okay. I gotta go," I said, waving good-bye.

That fall when school started, I was still too shy to talk to James. I ended up dating Grey, his best friend, because Grey talked to me first. Grey was straightforward and let me know he liked me. It was a decision I would live to regret.

"I like you, Nova," James had told me when I was eight months pregnant with Grey's baby.

Grey had picked me up so I could spend the night at his house. James was in the car. Grey stopped at Caravan convenient store to grab a juice, leaving the two of us alone. James took this opportunity to finally tell me how he felt. "I always liked you," he said. "But when I saw that you and Grey were kickin' it, I let ya'll do ya'llz' thang."

I turned to look at James. "I liked you too," I told him. "I wish you woulda said somethin' sooner."

James was silent. There was nothing to say. James remained a good friend to me. He was there when Grey left me down and out, but because I had a baby with Grey, I always felt obligated to Grey.

James and Grey fell out shortly after I turned eighteen. Unfortunately, Topaz hooked up with James shortly thereafter. I'd told Topaz about James long before they met. I didn't hate when Topaz told me she was talking to James, even though she knew the story.

"I was just trying ta get the pussy," James told her when she asked him about me.

Topaz knew all there was to know, so I left it alone. Now at twenty-three, I was being confronted with an old issue. James was a problem I couldn't escape.

* * *

I sat next to the friend that James had brought with him. I felt nervous. This was the first time the two of us had talked face-to-face since I'd seen James at the mall close to three years earlier back in early 2002.

During that time, Topaz and James had an on and off relationship. When I ran into James at the mall Topaz was with me. They had been broken up almost a year by then but I still felt in inappropriate to talk to him on a serious level.

We stood next to an earring booth and James and I chit-chatted back and forth while he made it a point to ignore Topaz. Jonathan was with me and James complemented me on the way I kept up with him. Jonathan had on new clothes and shoes and a fresh hair cut. It was obvious that even though Grey was out of the picture I was getting along just fine.

During the entire conversation, he refused to spare her one

word. I was happy to see James but uncomfortable about the circumstance. I thought about that moment often. I cannot think of how often I'd wished that Topaz wasn't there and I would have encountered James on my own.

I glanced at the boy next to me, glad he was there. He was tall and slender. He wasn't as attractive as James, but since he was there for me, I decided to be polite. He turned to face me. "Hi," he said.

Before I could answer, James cut in, "Don't talk to Nova," he said. "Nova is high maintenance. She don't talk to niggas like you."

"Ah, man," he said.

"Nova doesn't wanna talk to a nigga like you, so don't say shit to her."

"Nigga, fuck you," the boy said.

"Fuck you. You can leave. Nigga, don't nobody want you here."

I shot Topaz a shocked look. I wasn't sure if James was joking or not. This was not what I'd expected.

"Aiight then, I'm out." The boy stood to leave. James followed him to the door.

"Is he for real?" I asked Topaz.

"I told you he was crazy," she said.

Topaz had told me about James's violent outbursts and mean attitude, but I couldn't imagine it. The James I knew was nice and never yelled or cursed at people.

One time during an argument, he'd threatened to slap me. "I'm not your baby daddy," James had told me. "I'ma slap the fuck outta you. I told Grey how to handle you."

I hadn't taken James's comment seriously. I knew he would never hit me.

James came back into the living room and sat down. "Good, two women—I can handle that. I can handle the both of you." He looked over at me seductively. I turned away. "Ya'll been smokin'?" he asked.

"Uh huh," I said.

"Michael and Jamal was just here. We smoked with them," Topaz explained.

"Naw, ya'll need to smoke some of my weed. I got that good shit," he said. Then James looked at me. "I've been knowing you for awhile, Nova. I know you real well."

I looked at Topaz hard. She understood the look. It was her responsibility to keep him in line. He was her man, not mine. "You don't know her," she said.

"Yeah, you don't know me," I chimed in.

James was quiet for a while. "So why aren't you drinking yet?" he asked Topaz in a rude voice.

She gave no answer.

Feeling tired, I leaned over, resting my head on the arm of the sofa. That made Topaz uncomfortable. "You want a blanket," she demanded more than asked.

"Yeah, thanks," I said, taking the blanket.

I felt guilty, as if I had done something wrong. I knew that she didn't want me lying down in front of James. I didn't know what to do. I wished James would shut up.

I looked over at Topaz. She was sitting nearly on top of James, giving me a cold stare. I could tell she was insecure. I had just had my hair done three days earlier. This time I sported a style with braids in the front and a curly weave in the back. I had on a full face of makeup and was dressed in a pair of tight pants showing off my curvy body and a pair of high heels. I felt over dressed.

I sat quietly while James rolled a blunt. I was still high from the weed I'd smoked earlier. My thoughts were cloudy, but my senses were sharp. I noticed Topaz had an evil look in her eyes when she looked at me, a look that I'd never seen before.

Topaz wanted to give James the "Down Low" test. She had complained about a few DL comments he'd made. She began talking about DL men. "That nigga's gay," James said, after she told him a story.

"He doesn't take it up the butt; he likes to fuck men," she said.

"Awe, that ain't nothin then. He just like to stick it in the booty," James responded.

Topaz and I shot each other wide-eyed glances. We talked about his comment for some time afterward.

Topaz continued to watch me with that evil look. I wanted to feel comfortable, but I couldn't. I puffed on James's blunt a few times; then I decided to leave.

"All right, y'all, I'm heading home," I said.

"Already?" Topaz asked.

"Yeah, I'm tired, and I'm high."

James hadn't been there five minutes, and I was leaving. The blunt wasn't even out, and I was grabbing my purse.

He looked at me disappointed. "You sure you wanna leave?" he asked.

"Yeah, I'm tired and high."

Topaz walked me to the door. "All right, girl, hit me up," she said.

I got lost on the way home and could barely remember where I lived. It was in part because I was so high, but it was also because I couldn't get over what had just happened. Topaz had showed me another side of her. After that night, I knew our friendship had changed forever.

Topaz called me a few days later. I was sitting alone in my condo, bored and wishing that I had something to do.

"Hey, girl," she said.

"Hey. What's up?"

"Nothing. I'm just chillin'. I had so much fun last night. I threw a set, and James and Kristina came over, and we just drank and hung out."

"You threw a set and didn't invite me?"

"Oh, I didn't think that you had a babysitter," she said, trying to sound convincing.

I knew she was lying. The real reason she hadn't invited was that she didn't want me around James. I invited her to every party I threw, yet she never invited me to hang out. We didn't stay on the phone long. I was pissed.

Topaz threw several more sets. She always told me about them but made sure she always had an excuse as to why I wasn't invited.

It was hurtful. After the situation with Alyson, I had no friends. Topaz was my last friend left in Lansing, and I could see that our friendship was nothing but a fake. I didn't cut her off. She was my only friend. Instead, I pretended as if I wasn't bothered by then shun, even though I was.

I lost count of the days I spent alone in my condo wishing for friends. I had no one to visit, and it was rare that someone stopped by to visit me. But it was nothing compared to what was to come.

Chapter Two:
Under the Knife

In March 2005, I was still off work due to a shoulder injury. I worked as a production assembler for General Motors. I'd been off work since October 2004.

It was nice not having to awake to the annoying buzz of the alarm clock. I'd forgotten the feel of the winter sting as I briskly tried to brush snow and ice from my windshield so I could hurry and enter morning traffic.

I was relaxed and yet anxious. I knew that my life was about to change. I just didn't know what the change would be.

I was set to graduate from Lansing Community College in mid-May. As a single mother, I never expected to receive a college degree, and now that the time was near, I was more nervous than ever. Plus, my shoulder injury was becoming an ever-increasing negative factor in my life.

GM sent me to a shoulder specialist.

"You need surgery on the left shoulder," Dr. Wells, the surgeon, told me.

I looked at him in shock. Surgery wasn't what I was expecting. "What about injections?" I asked.

"You're past the stage of physical therapy and injections. Your bones are grinding together. You will have to have the bones shaved down." He looked over at me through his glasses. "I have a large scope with a camera and a laser on the end. I will make two small incisions here and here."

Dr. Wells pointed to the sorest places on my left shoulder. "I will scrape off part of the bone. There is a small vacuum on the end of the laser, so there will be no bone material left in your shoulder. The incisions are small. I don't use stitches."

Sensing my reluctance, Dr. Wells looked at me. "You don't have to go with me. There is one other doctor in the area that performs this operation. But he doesn't use a laser. He will make a long incision the length of your scapula, and he'll saw off part of your scapula with a saw. I'm the only surgeon who uses a laser," he said with pride.

I didn't want to be sawed on. The laser technique definitely sounded better. I told Dr. Wells I wanted him to perform my operation.

We scheduled my surgery for the week after my graduation. I wanted to be finished with the semester first. Sometimes I second guessed my decision to have surgery. I wondered if more therapy would work or if surgery was a definite. Yet the cracking and grinding continued and the pain was at a steady increase.

I was depressed thinking about my injury. I'd worked as a production assembler for the last five years of my life, and there wasn't a day that went by that I didn't pray for an out. Yet I never thought my out would come by way of extreme pain.

Some nights the ache crept from my shoulders and percolated down my arms and into my hands. Gliding through my muscles like a winding river, the pain struck at the most unexpected times. Sometimes it would come when I was sitting on the couch watching television or when I was taking a walk around the lake trail.

I hated the pain, and yet no amount of drugs could rid me of my affliction. Plus the cracking and grinding and my left shoulder was increasing daily. I knew I had no other choice. I decided to have the snapping scapula surgery performed on my left shoulder and then resume physical therapy on both.

I sulked around my condo in deep thought. I talked over the details of my surgery with my son, Jonathan, who was only seven years old at the time. He seemed to understand.

Fear slowly left me as I realized that the only thing I should be focused on was making sure I recovered in a timely manner so I could return to work as quickly as possible.

As much as possible, I pushed the details of my surgery to the back of my mind and focused on what was in front of me—graduation.

Chapter Three:
The First Walk

GRADUATION WAS HELD AT the Breslin Center in East Lansing. I knew that graduation was going to be huge if it was being held at the Breslin. The Breslin Center is one of the largest auditoriums in the area.

I arrived at the Breslin with Jonathan and my youngest brother, Green. The three of us were dressed to impress. The tan-colored slacks and butter yellow top I wore were concealed underneath my graduation gown. I felt chic and sophisticated.

Green looked handsome, dressed casually in a pair of dark khakis and a loose-fitting button-up. The olive green shirt he wore complimented his tan complexion.

Jonathan walked over to the drinking fountain and casually sipped water between two missing front teeth. He looked over at me and smiled. He looked nice in sneakers and loose-fitting jeans. His red hair lay down smoothly.

He looks just like me.

"Take Jonathan and find your seats," I told Green. "I have to figure out where I need to be."

I checked our tickets, and we proceeded through the large glass doors.

I looked around, trying to locate a familiar face. I saw no one I recognized. It was then that I realized this was a much different situation from high school graduation, where every face was a friend, either familiar or distant.

The Breslin Center was shaped like a large funnel with the performance stage located at the bottom and the seats at the top. You had to walk down a steep stairway to get to the stage. I never looked down when walking to my seat. I was afraid of heights.

As long as my guests had their tickets, they could sit anywhere they wanted. Green and Jonathan left to find seats close to the front. I was led into the basement and lined up with the other graduating students.

I had to stand among a thousand strangers, and yet I felt connected to them. I began a casual conversation with several of the people around me. We were all nervous and anxious to get started, yet we remained relaxed.

In unison, we were led out of the basement waiting room and over to our seats. I waited silently as different guest speakers gave us final words of encouragement. A comment that one of the last guest speakers made caught my attention.

"Every one of you who are about to graduate is here because someone helped you," he said.

At that moment, a man in the audience yelled out, "I raised you, boy."

A murmur of laughter erupted.

I laughed along with the crowd, and then my mind drifted. Questions began to float through my mind, along with some answers. What about the people who feel as if they weren't helped along their journey? Who gets credit for their successes? What about parents of successful children? Do they get the credit for their child's success?

To me, these questions spoke to the fundamental basis of contentment. How could someone feel complete if another person took his or her credit? After some thought, I decided that I didn't like either the speaker's comment or the comment the man in the audience had made.

My journey was a singular one. I'd paid for the help I had received and therefore disregarded their handouts as little more than mutual business transactions.

I refocused on the graduation ceremony, realizing that, in some way, I expected that Yellow, Earnest and perhaps my parents along with Green were listening would render themselves partly responsible for my accomplishment, and that left me somewhat unnerved.

There was something else I noticed while waiting for my row to stand. LCC announced all the students who had a 3.0 grade point average or higher. For the first time in years, I thought about my grades. I wished that I would have done better. My GPA was only a 2.3.

When I get my bachelor's, I am gonna come out with at least a three point, I promised myself.

Adrenalin rushed as my row stood to be called. I couldn't stop smiling as I walked across the stage. I knew that Jonathan was in the audience, and he was the only person there that truly mattered.

Besides Jonathan, I didn't think about who was there and who wasn't as I listened to my name being called. I smiled for my graduation picture, and waved to my family. (I'd spotted them while sitting down).

I sat back down after my name had been called and waited for the end of the graduation ceremony. I kept it to myself that I had one class to complete until I actually received my degree. I figured by the time everyone started asking about my degree, I would have finished the class anyway.

After we cleared out of the auditorium, the graduates were directed through a door that took us back into the basement and up the stairs. Once back in the hall, I had a chance to find my family.

"Congratulations," Green said, walking up to me.

He was with my eldest sister, Yellow; Donny, my nephew; and Earnest, my eldest brother.

"Thanks," I said.

"How does it feel?" Yellow asked.

"Great."

"Mom and Dad aren't here. They came late and left once they heard your name called," Yellow informed me. She looked at me curiously. "So what you gonna do now?"

I shrugged my shoulders. "I don't know. Want to go get something to eat?"

"Yeah. Let's go to Cheddar's," she said.

The six of us took a few more pictures with me in my cap and gown.

I left the Breslin Center excited and somewhat exhausted as I thought about the last class I had to complete.

The anxiety left me as I entered Cheddar's.

Cheddar's was my favorite restaurant. It was where I'd had my first date with Grey.

I'd nearly harassed Grey until he'd taken me out on an official date. We were young when we first met. He didn't even have a car. After a year, he had matured to the point that he had achieved automobile success. Now that he was an automobile driver, I demanded that he take me out on a date. He chose Cheddar's was the place he chose.

The six of us sat at a large square table in the back of the restaurant and chatted over the day's events. I was glad that we'd been placed in a quiet area. I tried not to think too much about the fact that my parents had stayed barely long enough to hear my name being called and my grandmother had decided not to show up at all.

My dad called me the next day to say congratulations. "Sorry I couldn't stay long," he said. "I did hear you name called though. I'm so proud of you."

"Thanks," I managed to mumble.

"I was talking to my mom, and we were trying to figure out why you stayed in school after you had your baby. She said that if you would have grown up in a big city, then you would have never graduated. I said it's because you had that baby and that kept you going. So which one is it?"

Here it was again—the age-old debate over small town versus big city. Did a child's location really matter? Even in Lansing, I had been exposed to it all—drugs, poverty, violence. Nothing was new to me.

A wave of frustration nearly escaped my closed lips. Instead of venting a useless argument, I let out a deep breath. "I don't know, Dad," I said.

"I told her that having that baby kept you going. So I guess it's a good thing you had him."

"I don't know," I repeated. "I would have stayed in school whether I had a baby or not," I said.

I knew where he was going. My family had decided not to support my decision to have my son at the tender age of sixteen. To punish my decision, they'd cut me off from all financial help, rendering me vulnerable to the stresses of life.

Despite the continuous setbacks, I'd still managed to pay my daycare, provide the necessary commodities for my son and me, and remain an active student. Despite the constant barrage of negative feedback from the family, I'd still managed to succeed, and that left them dumbfounded.

I knew there was a major debate brewing among the family. The graduation speaker's comment about all students having been helped along their journey had sparked a feeling of possession in some members. Those who'd had nothing to do with me completing college now wanted recognition.

I gave none.

I continued on with our conversation, not allowing myself to acknowledge his subtle boasting.

*   *   *

To celebrate my graduation, I decided to give myself an open house. I invited all my friends and family to join me for dinner and possibly give me a graduation gift.

I threw my open house at Fire Mountain the Sunday after graduation. I sent out over thirty invitations to various friends and family members.

Only a few people showed up. I shook off the feeling of rejection and enjoyed myself anyway.

Instead of focusing on who wasn't there, I focused on who

was. I laughed joked and enjoyed the fact that we were all gathered to celebrate my graduation. Grandma came this time.

We were all in good spirits, and my dinner went off without a hitch. I was glad. I had bigger things to worry about than petty competitions.

*   *   *

After graduation, it was time for my surgery I was nervous, even though the cracking and grinding in my left shoulder had become so intense that I prayed for my surgery. The date had been set for five days after graduation—May 17.

Grandma drove me to my surgery. I was going to go alone, but she cautioned against it. After listening to her reasoning, I agreed. It was too dangerous for anyone to go through surgery alone. Anything could happen on the operating room table, it was best to have family there in case something went wrong.

Dr. Wells performed my surgery at Ingham Regional Medical Center on Cedar Street in Lansing. Ingham was the smallest hospital in Lansing, which provided an element of privacy and serenity.

I arrived at Ingham prepared and calm.

We sat in the large waiting area while I filled out paperwork. The waiting area had three televisions, two comfortable couches, and several leather chairs. The carpet was soft and new. This was a definite divergence from the other two hospitals in the Lansing Area, Sparrow hospital and St. Lawrence Medical Center, where the hard floors and plastic chairs added no comfort to the inconvenience of being at a hospital.

I was escorted into a room with a bed, two leather chairs, and a television. I changed into my gown and waited for Dr. Wells. Grandma sat at my bedside, and we watched *Family Feud*. We busied ourselves by trying to come up with the answers.

When Dr. Wells came in, he was cheerful but more serious than he'd been during the previous times I'd met with him. He explained the procedure to me once more. Then he made two marks on my left shoulder with his marker.

"This is where I will go in," he explained. "I have a long laser with a camera on the end. I will scrape off part of the bone from each of these two locations. There are risks. I am only inches away from your lungs. If something goes wrong, I could puncture your lung."

Fear sprang into my eyes. I let out a silent breath and relaxed. I knew what had to be done. I nodded my head in understanding. I was scared, and I was ready.

The anesthesiologist came to administer the anesthesia. A nurse placed a gas mask over my nose. "Just take a deep breath," she told me.

I took a deep breath. After another breath, my body began to relax. I held out my hand for the anesthesiologist. The anesthesiologist inserted a needle into the largest vein in my right hand. The last thing I remembered was my grandmother rubbing my forehead.

I woke from surgery feeling groggy but only for a few seconds. A pain like I'd never felt before began to engulf me. First, it was soreness, and then it became an intense stinging. As I came around, I became more aware; and along with the burning, I felt as if I'd been torn apart—as if someone had sawed off my left arm.

"Morphine, please give me some morphine," I cried to the nurse.

The nurse got on the phone and made a phone call. "She's asking for morphine," she said. Then she glanced at me. "Yes, she's crying."

The nurse hung up the telephone. She went into a cabinet and began filling a needle. She gave me a shot in the leg. Immediately the pain began to subside. My fingers relaxed and went numb. My legs stop jerking up and down; they simply went limp and refused to move. I could breathe again. I took a deep breath and relaxed.

I'd left my body and my consciousness evaded me as my mind eased into a realm of the sublime. I felt so good I didn't want to come back into existence. I begged for more.

"May I have some more morphine, please?" I asked the nurse.

She gave me a stern look. "No, she said. "From now on, all you get is Vicodin."

I was moved to another waiting room, much like the first. Grandma had left, but my mom was there. Jonathan was with her.

I gave my son a kiss and was thankful that, thus far, I had survived my ordeal.

My mom kept Jonathan for me for the first four days after my surgery. I stayed in bed those first days, sleeping, thanks to the Vicodin. My shoulder bled constantly. Dr. Wells had told me that it would. He'd used no stitches to close me up.

I was alone most of the time. Yellow came to visit me once while I was recovering. She didn't help me around the house. Instead, she sat at the foot of my bed and watched me, a look of horror on her face, as if watching me wallow in pain somehow hurt her. She didn't stay long, just long enough to say that she'd stopped by.

After four days, my mom brought Jonathan back. I was still in a lot of pain, and I would have liked for her to keep him longer, but she wouldn't do it. That was the hardest part for me. Even disabled, I still had to take care of my child.

Jonathan was a good boy. He fixed himself something to eat and kept himself occupied. I stayed in bed.

By mid-June I felt good again. I was bored, and it occurred to me that I could write a book. My shoulders had healed to the point that I could sit for a limited time at a computer. I realized that I may never get another opportunity to do something I wanted.

I worked on my book throughout the summer. I talked it over briefly with the people around me. No one believed that I could accomplish something so great as to write a book. I didn't care about their lack of encouragement. I wrote my book anyway.

CHAPTER FOUR:
My New Best Friend

JUNE 14, 2005, WAS Jonathan's eighth birthday. One thing set this birthday apart from all the others—Grey was coming to the party. Grey and I had become friends a few weeks earlier.

I spent two days cleaning my house preparing for Jonathan's birthday party. I scrubbed every visible surface, making sure that every lint ball had been dusted away and every crumb vacuumed up. I even washed all the walls.

I invited all of the family, plus Kyle and Topaz my only two friends.

I'd met Kyle while working on the assembly line at GM. I was a new hire and he was the first friend I'd met. I worked on the heater hose which was my first permanent job at GM.

We worked next to each other for over a year. I ended up transferring to another job because I'd begun having problems with pain in my shoulders but we remained good friends.

I told no one that Grey was coming. Grey was unreliable. I didn't want to disappoint Jonathan by telling him that his dad was coming knowing there was a possibility Grey wouldn't show up.

Everyone arrived on time. Yellow and my grandma sat in the living room talking.

"Come help me blow up these balloons," I asked Yellow.

She looked at me and said, "I had to work overtime all week, and I'm tired. I just came over here to relax."

Yellow didn't bother to help. Instead, she talked with my grandma. The two of them sat in the living room while I continued to blow up balloons. Frustrated that I was running out of time, I quickly tried to get the rest of the balloons inflated so I could hang them up and move on to setting up the table.

Why is she so lazy?

I watched Yellow sit. Uninteresting, self-centered, and obnoxious, she actually took pride in her light complexion. She had a deep longing to be better than me, but she always came up short. She lounged on my couch, body squeezed into a tight pair of blue jeans, and tried to act sophisticated.

I ignored her cavalier behavior and proceeded with my party.

I didn't ask Grandma for help. She was old and had two bad knees from years of working on the assembly line at GM. I knew that she was too tired and in too much pain to help. Plus she looked like she didn't want to be bothered either.

"Here, give me some balloons," my mom said.

Mom, her pretty face still youthful grabbed several balloons from me.

"Thanks," I said, glad to have her there.

I shot another glance at Yellow. She tried to ignore my stare, yet I could tell by her body language that she felt my eyes piercing into the side of her face.

"You have a nice home," Grandma said, looking around.

"Thanks," I said.

I loved my condo.

I learned humility from having such a nice home. It was my prize. I had spent years working for it. I never compared my home to others; nor did I compare myself to others. I had arrived.

I finished hanging the balloons in the archway that separated the dining room from the living room just as Grey pulled up. All the children were outside playing in the front yard. From the window, we could see Grey giving Jonathan a hug.

"His dad is here?" Grandma asked me, surprised.

"Yeah, I invited him."

Yellow and Grandma exchanged confused looks and people were in a never-ending struggle to keep up. And so on this particular day, Grey had decided to make a change and show up for his son's eighth birthday.

I answered the door for Grey and reintroduced him to everyone. It had been so many years since he'd last seen my family that I felt an introduction was needed. The looks on everyone's faces were awkward. Even I felt somewhat unnerved, but I pushed those feelings aside and proceeded as if Grey had never been absent from our lives.

I was twenty-four years old now. In the seven years that I'd known Grey, I had learned many things. I'd learned that, no matter what the rest of the world thought, we would always be family. We were bonded by parenthood.

Grey said hello to everyone and then followed me to the dining room.

"What's up?" he asked me.

"Nothing, just trying to get this table together," I replied.

My frustration was beginning to show. "I was planning on taking all the kids swimming, but it's cold. I bought a piñata and some candy. I figured we would play games and bust the piñata."

Grey looked at the piñata and gave his nod of approval. "Is there anything you want me to do?"

"Grab that bag of candy and start filling up the piñata."

Before the opportunity passed, I grabbed my camera. "Hey, Grandma, would you mind taking a picture of us?"

Grey and I stood together smiling, our arms wrapped around one another as we posed for the picture. I wanted something definitive to show that he'd been there.

Grey stepped in and helped with the party. He grabbed the piñata and filled it with candy. Then he took it outside and hung it from the large tree in the front. To keep the kids busy, he played tag and a game called Red light/Green light with them.

"That's nice that his dad came," Grandma said.

"Uh-huh," I cautiously responded.

Grey had warned me not to say much about our relationship to my family. As young teenagers, we'd had so little control over the direction of our courtship. My family, vengeful and unwilling to compromise, had caused many issues to erupt between Grey and me.

At first, I didn't understand, but over time, I realized that support from family was a necessary component to building any strong relationship. Grey and I lacked support from our families, and therefore, we never learned to support each other. So for the first time, I followed my instincts and listened to my child's father, knowing that, in the long run, his advise was best.

After setting up the table, I went outside and took a few pictures of the birthday party. Despite the cold wind and the dreary skies, it was a beautiful day. I watched Grey smile and laugh as he raced back and forth with the kids. My neighbor came outside to chat with me for a while.

I enjoyed talking with Lezzy. I rarely saw her, and I took this as an opportunity to break the ice. In addition, I wanted to ensure her that my party wasn't too much of a distraction. Since we lived so close to one another, I tried to be as courteous as possible.

Grey gave Jonathan forty dollars for his birthday.

Unfortunately, Grey had to leave the party before we could cut the cake and ice cream.

"I told Cherry I was going up to my job to check on a fax and then I was going to the store. She'll be wondering where I am by now," Grey said, as he gave me a hug good-bye.

Cherry was Grey's girlfriend of five years. Cherry and I weren't friends. She had her life and her relationship with Grey, and we stayed out of each other's way.

I was bothered by the fact that Grey had to lie just to go to his son's birthday party.

Why can't you tell your girlfriend that you're going to your son's birthday party? That is so crazy. Why do you have to lie to see your own kid?

Grey's fear of telling people the truth about his life and his feelings was his biggest flaw. Early in a relationship, you teach your partner how to treat you. I believed that Grey had failed at training Cherry. In my opinion, he should have been able to bring

Cherry along to the party with no dispute. Yet, since he'd failed in his obligations as a father, all he could do was lie to her and hope she didn't find out.

We sung Jonathan "Happy Birthday" and cut the cake. Jonathan had a continuous smile on his face as he went through his birthday presents. I was satisfied as a mother that my job for the day had been completed.

Another birthday meant another year had past. We'd completed another cycle around the sun. Jonathan was officially one year older.

"This is one of the best birthday parties I've ever thrown," I told my mom.

"We never went anywhere for ya'lls birthday. We always had a good time cutting cake and ice cream at home. Those are the best parties—the ones you have at home," Mom said.

I agreed.

After the birthday party, Grey came by to visit me just about every day. He worked just five minutes away from me, and since he was a loan officer, he could leave his job whenever he wanted. The only days we didn't see each other were on the weekends.

Grey never spent more than a minute or two with Jonathan during his visits. His main purpose for coming over was to see me. Grey patted Jonathan on the head, asked him how he was doing, and then headed upstairs with me.

As a mother, I made a terrible judgment call. Looking back so many years later, I see that allowing Grey to have a relationship with me but not his son was a mistake.

I should have put a stop to my friendship with Grey right then. I saw that he wanted the benefits of a family with me without the responsibility of being involved. Thinking that friendship could make a parent out of him and ignoring the warning signs of impending disaster, I continued on with our relationship.

Grey and I spent the majority of our time talking. Grey had been out of my life for over four years. Tired of the person he was, Grey had made a drastic change at the age of twenty-two. He'd wanted a new life, and he'd gotten it. The only problem was that, now, he wanted pieces of his old life back—an impossibility.

After a few weeks, I realized that one the pieces of his life that Grey wanted back was his control over me. That's how it had been with us. Back in high school, I had nearly worshipped him. I'd followed him on a daily basis. I'd called him more than an athlete chases a win.

I knew that Grey was making no plans to include Jonathan in his life. Despite the fact that he saw me every day, he still lied to Cherry. He went to great lengths to make sure that she didn't suspect anything. And I went to great lengths to protect him.

In reflection, I can that my decision to do so was flawed. At the time, I thought that my relationship with Grey was more important than his relationship with Cherry; after all, he shared a child with me and had no such obligation with Cherry.

In my mind, that put me ahead of her. In reality, Grey shouldn't have been focusing on Cherry or me. He should have been focusing on Jonathan. Any man who had to lie to conceal that he was in the picture wasn't worth having around. But it would take me years to accumulate that knowledge. In the mean time, I continued on without regard to Jonathan's feelings or my own.

By the end of the summer, my relationship with Grey had grown; we were each other's best friends. And he *was* my best friend. I told him everything about me, and he did the same.

We enjoyed going on long drives out into the country. Sometimes Jonathan was away visiting my mom; sometimes Green was at my house and watched him.

On our drives, we talked about our life's dreams. "Look at that house," Grey would say as he pointed to a country mansion. "I wonder about the people that live there. They don't even realize how good they're livin'."

I agreed. No one knew how well they were doing at the time. People only appreciate the good times when they're over.

I stared at the houses. Each was beautiful and different, like the memories I'd been reflecting on.

It was as if the structures had appeared by magic, as if by the wave of a wand, a string of castles had appeared from a landfall, each sheltering its inhabitants as a mother cradles her newborn. A spiritual a gift from God himself, a home represented, to me, imaginable wealth. I started at each house and was happy for the people who lived there.

Grey wanted to leave Lansing and start over someplace else. He had made many mistakes in his youth, and as time progressed, his past had become a smothering blanket.

I just wanted to find happiness. As time wore on, my condo was not enough to satisfy me. An emptiness surrounded me—I had a purpose that remained unfulfilled. I knew that there was something out there for me, and it was only a matter of time before I would pull my anchor up and leave to find it.

By the end of the summer, I was spending the majority of my time with Grey. He had become my life.

CHAPTER FIVE:
So You Wrote Your First Book?

I FINISHED MY BOOK in September. Finishing my book was a transformation for me. I had done something great, and I knew it. My book was called *Diamonds in the Rough*. I'd taken the title from a hair salon that I'd visited and loved during my childhood.

Diamonds in the Rough was about three sisters who were all going through a difficult time in their lives. Their names were Sabrina, Simone, and Michelle.

Each of the girls was plagued with inner turmoil (as most people are in this world). What made these girls different from most people was that they were unafraid to branch out and at least try to find themselves.

Sabrina and Simone were both light complected and beautiful yet suffered from extreme low self-esteem. Why did I describe the characters in this way? The reason was simple. I wanted to show the black community and the rest of the world that light-skinned people face the same issues of inadequacy as everyone else.

I also gave Sabrina and Simone short, kinky hair, while Michelle, my dark-skinned character, sported a long, silky mane. I did this to prove that jealousy rests in all women for all reasons. Sabrina and Simone teased Michelle constantly because of her dark skin yet loathed her because of her hair.

Looking in the mirror, none of the girl's was happy with her reflection. Each wanted what the other had. And that is how it was in real life. Most people found being satisfied with their own blessing difficult.

When I wrote about the girls feeling inadequate because of their African hair, I based those feelings on my own experience. I had always wished for long, silky hair. I had learned through life,

43

though, that being satisfied with oneself was important. Like my characters, over time, I learned to accept my own beauty.

I gave Michelle long, silky hair to signify that everyone has something unique—something that makes him or her special—and that is what's important. If not long, silky hair then Michelle would have had a beautiful shape, a sparkling personality, or a remarkable talent—something to show that God gave everyone a special gift.

Writing my book was a way for me to express the feelings I could never say. I hoped that other women would read my book and relate to the characters. I was careful as to how close I got to the characters. I didn't want to expose myself. I purposely added in scenes and characters and thoughts that were far away from the real me and my experiences. The detachment made me feel safe.

I sent my book in to be copy written by the Federal Copy Write office before I sent it to different publishing companies. I sent my book to every publishing company I could find. I even sent *Essence* magazine an e-mail explaining that I had just finished writing my first book and asked for information about how to get it published.

I'll never know if they read my e-mail, but in the next month's issue there was an article entitled "So You Wrote Your First Book." The article contained helpful tips for new authors on getting published and included an interview with a top agent in the business. Along with the agent's expert advice, the article listed the names of some book agents.

In my heart, I believed *Essence* had published that article specifically for me.

I found one company that would publish my book, Publish America. Upon researching, I learned that Publish America was a self-publishing company. Publish America didn't require authors to pay for their books up front. Rather, the company printed the books for free. The more copies sold, the more books Publish America published.

I jumped for joy when I got the acceptance letter. It was

my first acceptance letter. Every other agency or publisher had rejected my book.

Then I read an Internet blog about Publish America that derailed my enthusiasm. The blogger wrote that she'd sent her book to Publish America and the company had agreed to publish her book. The only problem was that Publish America published everyone's book. As a joke and to test this theory, a friend of the woman sent in a book. The book was filled with the same word over and over. Publish America sent the blogger's friend an acceptance letter.

I didn't want to go with Publish America. I wanted a publisher that would give me an advance.

Asia, my older sister by a mere one year, gave me the number of a book publisher in New York. I called him to see what I could do.

"What I am is a distributor," he told me. "I am the largest distributor of African American books on the East Coast. What you need to do is get your book published—either find a publishing company or self publish. Once you get a book in print, call me, and we'll make it happen."

Ironically, during this time, a famous writer was coming to Lansing. I'd never heard of him before. The announcers at Power 96.5 gave Eric Jerome Dickey rave reviews.

Dickey would arrive in Lansing on Saturday, September 30, 2005, to accept a literary award from the Michigan Literary Council.

I must go see him. I have to know how he got his start.

I left the house thirty minutes early. I arrived at the Lansing Center located in downtown Lansing fifteen minutes before the award ceremony was scheduled to start. After a quick hunt, I found a parking spot around the corner from the Lansing Center. I walked though a set of large, glass doors separating the elegant Lansing Center from the noisy strip club across the street.

I walked into one of the main ballrooms in the Lansing Center. Ninety percent of the seats were taken. There had to be over three hundred people waiting to hear Dickey speak. There were a few seats left in the front row located on the left side of the podium.

I slid into the seat close to the entrance door. I admired the floor-length curtains hanging behind the podium. The matching carpet with the Picasso design entertained my eyes.

The reading started promptly at seven.

A large black woman in a free-flowing skirt introduced Dickey. "He has written over ten novels, including the best-seller, *Liar's Game*, and *Lovers and Friends*," she said.

Why haven't I heard of him? He has all those books out, and I've never heard of him, I thought.

The introduction continued. Then Dickey was asked to come out. The audience grew silent as Dickey entered the room. He had brown skin, dreadlocks, and a confident attitude. Dickey commanded attention as he approached the stadium. His relaxed smile put the audience at ease.

He gave a brief introduction. "Thank you all for coming this evening. I'm honored to accept this award."

After his thank you speech, Dickey read a few pages from the latest novel he was working on. It was entitled *Chasing Destiny*. The passage started out steamy. A confrontation between two women in a public restaurant began the story. Immediately, I became interested. Yet it became difficult to concentrate once a baby in the back of the room began to cry.

Who the hell brings a baby to a book reading? Whoever the parent is knows they're ultra ghetto, I thought.

An interruption occurred when a cell phone went off. Dickey continued reading ignoring the cell phone. "Keith, you know I love you and want to be with you. Then a cell phone rang," Dickey read in an even tone, the audience remained captivated until Dickey laughed and said "Man, I'm good."

I laughed along with the audience.

I like this guy. He's funny. I bet whoever left their cell phone on wishes they woulda turned it off.

I continued listening to his story. I was entranced. His voice was smooth, clear, and melodic. I let out a loud groan along with the rest of the audience when Dickey stopped reading. He was at a good part, and we wanted him to continue. But he didn't. He gave us just enough to keep us wanting more.

Next, it was time for the Q&A. My palms began to sweat. Once I'd learned Dickey lived in LA and was a million-dollar writer, my nerves had left me. I had never spoken to a celebrity before. I didn't want to embarrass myself. A part of me wanted to remain silent.

Say something. You came all this way. You better say something. You've been trying for months to get published; this may be your only chance to learn the game from someone who's in it.

I raised my hand. He looked at me and nodded for me to speak.

"Hi, this question has nothing to do with your work. I wanted to know—how did you first get published?" I asked.

"It took me five years to get published," Dickey told me. "I got rejection letter after rejection letter, but I kept working on it. I was working as an engineer. Then I got laid off. I started writing while I was off. I went back to school. As I learned, I went back and added in the things I learned. It was hard because, even after my book got accepted, I still had to wait. Terry McMillan was coming out with a new book. The publishing company didn't my book to come out at the same time and have to compete with hers. I wanted to hurry up and get my book out there. I was ready to start getting royalties."

The audience laughed.

I feel ya. Who ain't ready to get paid?

I raised my hand again. "What about self publishing?"

"Self publishing can be a good start. However, the critics don't recognize self-published authors. What I did was go to book conventions. It was difficult standing there among all the other authors, and people are walking by, like 'Eric Jerome Dickey, who's that?' You have to sell yourself and let people know why you stand out from the others."

I stared at him hard. I tried to remember everything he said, word for word. This was a chance I knew I would never get again.

Dickey had one last piece of advice. "The main thing you want to do is go to school. Learn the craft," he said.

Dickey had to move on and take another question. That was one of my proudest moments. I did what I'd set out to do. I talked to Eric Jerome Dickey and learned about the writing industry.

After the Q&A ended, I hurried to purchase one of Dickey's books. I decided to go with *Genevieve*, his latest novel at the time. By the time I purchased the book, the line to get an autograph was long. I could have waited around, so I'd be the last person to talk to him, but I left. I hadn't come for an autograph. I'd come for information.

I continued to search for a publisher. I opted not to go with self publishing because the companies I'd explored didn't offer editing and I needed an editor. Even as a new writer, I knew my work needed editing. I looked up editors on the Internet, but it would cost roughly$1,500 to $2,000 to have a professional edit my book.

I became discouraged. I tried not to talk about my book, which was all my family and friends could talk about, that is, everyone but Topaz. She said nothing when I told her I'd finished writing my book. I didn't expect her to.

By this time I had come to realize the jealousy that Topaz felt for me. It was the same problem I'd experienced with Allyson and a slew of other friends and so I ignored her.

I discovered another problem with my book when I googled the name *Diamonds in the Rough*. It turned out that the title had already been taken. I had to come up with a new name fast. All the names I thought of with the word *diamond* had been taken. It seemed everybody loved titles about diamonds.

My friend, Jonah, suggested that I call the book *If a Heart Had Eyes.*

I'd met Jonah when I transferred into the paint department at GM. I was twenty-three at the time and had just finished another round of physical therapy and restrictions with my job. I transferred to the paint department to give my shoulders a rest since the jobs in the paint department tended to be easier than the ones on the main assembly line.

Jonah and I hit it off from the start. We had a lot in common; our birthdays were only days apart making him a Taurus like me. He had a light brown complexion and soft eyes that were warm and inviting. He wore his head shaved bald and wore shirts that showed off his six pack.

Immediately I trusted Jonah and invited him to my house. I was having computer problems at the time and he was a big help in helping clear out my computer. Jonathan seemed to like him and since Jonah had children around the same age as Jonathan, he seemed like a good role model.

I liked the title and thought it was unique. I told him I would use it. I didn't like using someone else's title for my work, but I thought it worked for the story.

Jonah was my biggest fan. He encouraged me every day. "You know what you need to do," Jonah advised. "You need to start working on another book right now. While you're waiting to get that book published, start working on another one."

At the time, I was out of new book ideas so I busied myself by editing my first book. However, every time I went back in to edit, the book grew in length. It went from 270 pages to 320. By the time I stopped editing, my book was over four hundred pages long. I desperately needed an editor.

CHAPTER SIX

Collegiate Quest

IN JANUARY 2006, A thought occurred to me, while I was dressing for school one day. Although I had already graduated and received my degree I was still taking classes at LCC. Unsure of what to do with my life, I floated around the small campus trying to figure things out.

In January 2006, I was getting dressed for school one day when it occurred to me that this was my last semester at LCC. I already had my degree and I'd finished all my classes. What was I sticking around for? *You're scared*, I told myself.

I couldn't let that stop me. I decided right then and there that I would make a change in my life. I wanted bigger success. I wanted my bachelor's degree.

I began submitting college applications online. By February of that year, I had been accepted at two schools—Central Michigan University and Western Michigan University. I'd also applied to Ferris and was in the process of looking for more schools.

For some reason, I never applied to Michigan State University, the local university. I think I already knew that I wanted to leave Lansing. Besides, I felt that there would be too many distractions to deal with if I attended State.

I'd always dreamed of becoming a Spartan. I knew, however, that what I would need was support or at least peace of mind. At that time in my life, I wasn't getting either and so leaving to go off to college was my game plan.

Once I got my acceptance letters from Western and Central, I stopped looking for colleges. All I needed was one school. Besides, I wanted to stay in Michigan.

Grey was one of the first people I told about my decision to attend school. He came to my house for a visit one day, and I was so excited I could barely sit down. As soon as he walked through the door, I was ready to share my good news.

"I'm so happy for you," Grey said.

"Thanks. At first I was gonna commute back and forth from Lansing, but then I got to thinking. I should move. I should move to the city of whatever school I choose while I go to school. It's looking like I won't be going back to work. All I have here is my condo, and I can always sell that or rent it out. I don't want to be in Lansing anymore. I have no friends here, no man. I always wanted to go off to college. That was my dream."

"You should do it. Have you decided which one you want to go to?"

"No. I know that Central is in Mt. Pleasant, and Western is in Kalamazoo, but I've never been to either of those cities."

"I'm gonna take you there," Grey said, looking me in the eye.

"Really?"

"Yeah, I want you to leave. There's nothing in Lansing. Let me make some arrangements with my job and Cherry. We'll make a day of it. We'll drive to one school, check it out, and go see the other."

"Thanks."

I told everyone that I had been accepted at the two schools. "Congratulations," I heard over and over. I still hadn't made my plans for leaving Lansing known. I wasn't sure which city I would choose.

I knew something was about to happen in my life because I'd begun having dreams that I was in college in a new city. The dreams had started in early 2005.

One dream was so real that I could feel the wind when it blew and smell the exhaust of the cars. In this dream, I lived on campus with Jonathan. There were several trails around the campus, and I liked to walk on the trails. The school was packed, and thousands of students hustled to and fro.

At one particular part of the dream, I stopped and talked to a white lady while out on a hike on one of the trails with Jonathan. The school was brick and had a lot of greenery.

Yeah, right. Me going off to college, I thought to myself when I awoke from the dream.

I lay in bed thinking over my vision—about how I'd felt strolling around campus with my son by my side. In my dream I was at peace. Happy with myself and my life, I felt that I had made it. My son was with me and that was serenity. We were together while I fulfilled my dream. To me it was honorable to have him there. I felt free.

At this school, I was accepted and had friends; unlike high-school where most days no one even bothered to speak to me. I was a baby-momma, Grey's baby-momma to be exact, and that made me an outcast.

The dream made me think of a life I'd longed to live—a person I'd wished to be.

College was a privilege, not a right. No one was born knowing that they would go to go to college or attend their school of choice. So when I got my acceptance letter, I said a prayer of thanks. Even if I never made it, just having the letter was an accomplishment.

Grey and I made arrangements to visit the schools on March 7. We planned to leave early in the morning while Jonathan was at school. Green would watch him after school if I was gone a long time. I was excited and scared, but I was ready for my new life.

* * *

"This is so exciting," I said to Grey as I closed and locked my condo's front door. I walked down the stairs and headed to the passenger side of my Cadillac CTS. "It's starting to get warm. I think this is gonna be a hot summer. I can't wait for the summer. I'ma be spending it in my new city."

I was still smiling as I climbed inside my car. Grey was driving that day.

Grey suggested we go to Central Michigan first and then drive to Western Michigan.

Central was located about an hour north of Lansing in the city of Mt. Pleasant. Mt. Pleasant was known for its casinos and nothing else.

My Uncle Marcus lived in Mt. Pleasant at the time, so if I moved there, I would have family in the city.

I didn't like the drive to Central. Halfway through the drive, the speed limit changed and we could only do 55 miles per hour.

Grey told me, "Be careful at this part. I used to come up here to the casino all the time. The police are always waiting, trying to get people 'cause they know most people don't slow down for the speed limit change."

On the way to Central, we spotted four police cars hiding along the side of the road at different checkpoints.

If I come here, I bet I'll end up with a ticket before the year is out.

I told Grey about my dream and what I'd thought when I'd first woken up from it. "Now look at me," I said.

"You're meant to do somethin'. I look at our lives like a movie being played. All the people we used to know. You know how, at the end of the movie, you get to the part that tells what happened to everybody? Your ending is gonna be good." Grey looked at me and smiled. "She left Lansing and went to college. Then she went on to write books. I'm proud of you."

I couldn't stop smiling. Happiness engulfed every inch of my being. My shoulders didn't hurt. My knees ceased to ache. Even my toes felt good. I bounced my feet up and down as I looked out the window.

Ice had begun to melt from the trees. I could feel the sun trying to find me from behind the clouds. I looked up at the grayish blue sky. The chill of winter was gone. Omnipresent spectrums of joy swallowed me up us as we drove.

I'm starting a new life. Everything that has happened to me is in the past. It's over. I made it. I'm going off to college, I thought.

Seeing CMU made my dream real; that I would go away to college seemed plausible, even probable. I knew it was going to happen. My eyes grew large as I looked upon the football stadium. The stands and the perfectly manicured lawn drew me in. I could imagine myself walking around campus in my Central Michigan tank top and yoga pants.

Central was beautiful. Each building was well maintained and cared for. Mt. Pleasant was a clean city, and everything surrounding Central was updated. I saw no abandoned houses or buildings, no stray children hanging out in the streets. Central had a suburban feeling.

Because of the cold temperature and snow still outside, most of the students were inside the buildings. We didn't stop on campus. We kept driving to see what else was out there.

"Their stadium is nice," Grey commented.

We continued past the college and headed into the city. Grey only drove down the main streets, careful not to get us lost. We were on a strict time schedule, and so every minute counted. I still wanted time to check out Kalamazoo. Neither Grey nor I had been there before.

"I know. I love it here. I can't wait to go to a game," I said, as I looked around. "This is so exciting. I woulda never thought I would be going off to college."

Grey smiled. "I can't wait for you to go. You and Jonathan should tailgate. It's fun. Cherry and me do it all the time."

"Yeah we should. I've never done that before."

The drive to Kalamazoo from Mt. Pleasant was long. I slept through most of it. We left Mt. Pleasant at close to eleven o'clock and didn't arrive in Kalamazoo until quarter after two. I awoke soon after we passed the sign that announced Kalamazoo in 16 miles.

"I'm hungry," I told Grey.

"We'll stop and get something once we get to Kalamazoo."

"Okay."

"What's the directions say?" he asked.

I grabbed the MapQuest directions we'd printed. "Get off at the downtown Kalamazoo exit; then follow 94 West. Stay on business loop 94. That should take us there. The directions say keep to your left."

To get to Western, we had to drive through downtown Kalamazoo. Grey and I looked around the city in surprise.

"The downtown is a lot bigger than Mt. Pleasant's. I don't think Mt. Pleasant even had a downtown. And look, there's a lot more black people here," Grey said.

"Yeah, there is."

Grey and I had seen only one other black person the entire time we were in Mt. Pleasant. I was used to white people. Lansing is predominately white. However, there was a black community in Lansing and several black sections. It didn't take long to find us.

I liked downtown Kalamazoo. There were several large buildings, not as big as the ones in New York, perhaps only ten to fifteen stories high. A large brick structure in the shape of a semicircle with a water fountain and stone letters that read "Kalamazoo" welcomed us into the city.

"Go left and stay to your left," I told Grey.

We continued driving. People mingled about the city. Despite the cold, homeless people still walked up and down the street.

"Look. There's the sign that says Western," I yelled to Grey, so excited that my voice had risen three octaves. "Okay, now go straight."

Kalamazoo was a city that had a lot of one way streets. Without warning two-way streets turned into one-way streets with different names. Grey and I experienced this for the first time. We went from being up the street from WMU to "lost" in an instant.

Grey looked around frustrated. "I thought you said go straight."

"The sign said Western Michigan University, and it had an arrow that pointed straight," I argued back.

He shook his head at me. I passed him a friendly smile. There was no use debating.

We decided to use the time that we were lost to get a good look at and get the feel of the city. The houses were beautiful. Bricks paved the streets. Many of the lawns were professionally landscaped.

I got a relaxed feeling driving around Kalamazoo. I felt as if I knew I would be living there. I relaxed in my seat. I knew Providence was stepping in.

"There it is," I said excitedly, barely able to contain my smile. "It's just like the school I saw in my dream."

Grey gave me a "whatever" look. I'd said that Central was the school in my dream when I'd first seen it. Now that I was looking at Western, I was convinced that WMU was the school I'd dreamed about.

The buildings were the same as the ones in my dream—brown brick surrounded by lots of greenery. And I had that feeling; I just knew. A time comes in everyone's life when his or her purpose calls. I couldn't run from my destiny. I was meant to be a Bronco.

We entered campus. WMU's campus was enormous. We drove down a long, winding road that cut through a forested area. Hundreds of trees lined the edge of the sidewalk. The trees stopped, and a large pond appeared.

"That's so pretty," I said, as I gazed upon the large pond.

I marveled at the arched wooden bridge that crossed over to the other side of the pond. Ducks sat at the pond's edge or wandered around in the tall grass.

Across from the pond was a parking lot and then buildings, the buildings sat atop a large hill overlooking the pond. A winding stairway led up to the buildings. Later in life I would have to climb those stairs on a regular basis and walk down that winding road to get home.

We continued along the winding road as it led us deeper into the heart of campus.

"This must be the main strip," Grey said.

"Yeah, you're right."

Hundreds of students hurried to and fro. They didn't stop or wait before they crossed the street. They walked right in front of us, never looking to see if we'd stopped or slowed down.

"These people are crazy. They don't even look," I said, as Grey had to break hard for a white girl who'd just walked out in front of us.

Later, I would learn that that was the way Western students operated. They figured that the driver was responsible to watch out for the pedestrian. In a lot of ways, that was the truth, although everyone was responsible for his or her own safety.

Grey pointed out that the football stadium was smaller than Central's. "This school must not put as much emphasis on sports," he figured.

I wasn't disappointed. To me, the stadium, which was still large and in excellent condition, was the right size. I wasn't a sports fan anyway. If I did get into a sport, it was boxing. On rare occasions, I watched the Super Bowl. I looked at the stands and imagined Jonathan sitting next to me on the bleachers cheering for our team.

Grey and I grabbed something to eat at the Burger King we passed on our way back to the highway.

"Thank you for bringing me here. I don't think I would have done it on my own," I told Grey as we sat in the parking lot eating.

"I knew you wouldn't. That's why I brought you."

After eight hours of driving and sightseeing, Grey and I made it back to Lansing. We smoked a blunt and talked before he headed back home. By this time, Cherry was putting in twelve hour days working and going to school at Ross Medical School. Grey loved it. He got to spend all day and evening with me.

"The only thing I don't like about my life right now is that I'm lonely," I told Grey. I took a long drag on the blunt and passed it.

"Even if you had someone, you could still be lonely. You know the worst feeling? Feeling lonely and having someone right next to you. Sometimes I'm lying in the bed with Cherry, and I feel so alone." Grey looked at me with sadness in his eyes.

That's because she doesn't know you. You're Grey Davis. But you can't be Grey Davis, or she'll leave.

"I know how you feel."

I had been in a bad relationship once with a person who'd done nothing but drone on and on about his ex-girlfriend. At first, I'd tried to be a listening ear, but over time I grew detached and unhappy. When I tried to talk to my boyfriend about these issues, he only complained. Over time, I became lonely even though we lived together.

The relationship was a nightmare, and I learned why people shouldn't hook up with someone they had nothing in common with.

I explained this to Grey as he drove. I told him about the times when I'd lay in bed all night thinking only of him, even though the spot next to me was filled.

Grey looked over at me. Our eyes met. We knew the truth. I had never gotten over him, and he'd never gotten over the life he left behind, which included me.

"I don't know. I feel obligated to Cherry. After that shit happened, you know my court case. My life was devastated. I didn't talk to no one. She was the only one around. She stayed holed up in the house with me twenty-four hours a day ..."

Grey made a sad and embarrassed face at me. I knew Grey didn't want to talk about his court situation. In his teenage years and his younger twenties Grey had been a man of the streets. He had to get out of the game and that meant turning in a longtime friend. According to him it was a hard decision. He'd told me that he did it because of his family's future. He must not have been thinking about Jonathan because after that I didn't see him anymore. He'd simply disappeared out of our lives. If I hadn't taken the time to find him again he would have been gone forever.

"I understand, but that isn't a normal life. She met you at a time when you had to cut everyone off and be with just her. That isn't normal. Couples don't just sit under each other like that."

"I know." Grey stared out the window. "Cherry always said that I needed her to make it. I have three felonies and almost a thousand dollars a month to pay in child support. Her only working part time while she goes to school and me paying all the bills showed me that I can make it on my own. I pay all the bills … without her help."

"You don't need anyone to survive. You never needed her. For as long as I've known you, you've always been under some girl. You've never been by yourself."

Grey looked at me surprised. He thought for a moment. "I've never been alone. Right after you, I was with Tamika, and after her, Cherry. Even in high school, I had a girlfriend before you."

"If you and Cherry don't work out, you should be alone for a while before you get into another relationship," I advised.

Grey nodded his head.

I hoped he was listening. He deserved, in fact needed, the opportunity to express his true self. How could he be happy in his relationship if he felt he was only there out of need? I wanted to reach out to him, but I knew I couldn't. It was a lesson he had to learn on his own.

Grey and I hugged good-bye in silence. I thanked him again for the college tour. Our conversation had unlocked the truth. Now he had to go home.

I went back to Central one last time. This time, I brought Green and Jonathan with me. We stopped by Uncle Marcus's house while we were there. I didn't like the vibe with Uncle

Marcus. I wasn't in the mood to deal with more family, so I accepted Western's offer.

I made arrangements to put my house on the market on April 1, 2006. Originally I planned to leave in August and start school in the fall semester. After giving it much thought, I decided that the sooner I got started, the better. I pushed my start date to June so I could begin the second semester of summer school.

I received my acceptance letter from Ferris as well, but I decided not to go for a visit. I liked WMU, and I wanted to go there.

CHAPTER SEVEN:
A Lansing Finale

ON MAY 1, 2006, I celebrated my twenty-fifth birthday. I wanted to do something different. I booked a hotel room online at the Red Roof Inn in Kalamazoo. I wanted to go out clubbing in my new city for my birthday. I would be moving to Kalamazoo in six weeks, and wanted to get broken in.

But something terrible happened. Jonathan burned his face and neck two days before my birthday. I still went to Kalamazoo for my birthday, though. I didn't want Jonathan's injury to stop my birthday celebration altogether.

Instead of shaking my booty at the club, I checked into my room with my son. We ordered a pizza from Domino's, watched movies, and played video games on his PS2.

I was ecstatic. I realized that the best days are those that you spend with the people who you are the closest to. There was no way I was leaving my son behind, and once we checked into the motel, I realized that I had made the right choice.

"Are you having fun on your birthday?" Jonathan asked me.

He munched on a piece of pizza and looked guilty about being there. I wanted him to know that, despite his injury, I was having one of the best days of my life.

We were together in our new city getting ready to branch out on our own. It was perfect.

"Yes, this is one of my best birthdays," I told him. "I'm in my new city with my son. We're hanging out at the hotel."

Jonathan looked sad. "You sure you want to be with me?"

"Yes, baby, I'm sure."

"Is it because of my face?"

I looked at the swollen blisters on his right cheek and the

large bandage on his chest that covered his boiled flesh. He was hideous, almost a creature—something that only a mother could love.

That's why I'd brought him. I didn't want anyone else taking care of him while he was hurt. I knew my family. The only place for my son was with me. It was as if his injury had brought us closer together. I had always taken him for granted, and seeing him hurt reminded me of how fragile life was.

I looked at Jonathan and said, "Yes, I didn't want to leave you when you were hurt. Besides, I'm having a great time with you."

I grabbed another slice of cheese pizza and took a bite. Jonathan smiled and continued playing his game.

*   *   *

I tried not to look at Jonathan or think about his burn. I blamed myself.

"Mom, can I make a bowl of Ramen noodles?" Jonathan had asked me two mornings ago.

Normally I didn't allow Ramen noodles for breakfast … but for some reason, I said yes. I didn't think anything of letting him prepare the noodles himself. He was almost nine at the time.

I heard the hum of the microwave, then the click of the microwave door being opened, and suddenly a loud scream. I jumped off of the couch and ran into the kitchen, thinking, *No. Oh God, please don't let it be anything I can't handle.*

I saw Jonathan convulsing. Large boils and blisters were forming on his face. I grabbed a cold towel. It wasn't until I turned back around and looked down at him that my stomach turned.

The skin on his chest was peeling away in layers. I knew what I had to do. I grabbed my car keys and threw on my shoes. No morning shower, no fresh makeup—we were going to the hospital.

I rushed around in a panic.

Jonathan tried to calm me down. "I'm fine," he said.

"You're not fine. Those burns look bad. I gotta get you to the hospital. Come on. Let's go."

I helped Jonathan ease into the car. He didn't cry, but he continued to shiver. I ran a red light and slowed down.

Don't get yourself in a car accident on your way to the hospital. Calm down. Slow down. Be careful. Drive safely.

I arrived at Sparrow Hospital, the place of Jonathan's birth. I walked up to the receptionist. She was already talking with another gentleman who had a cut on his hand. "My son needs medical attention," I said, cutting the man off.

They looked at Jonathan.

"You go ahead. He looks like he needs it more than me," the man said.

"Thank you."

I was grateful for the man's generosity.

Jonathan was rushed into a room. The doctors cut off his shirt and went to work. They looked at me funny because I kept requesting pain medication for him. I didn't care. I didn't stop my request until the anesthesiologist arrived. I didn't want my son to be in pain.

I stayed at the hospital all day with Jonathan. Grey stopped by for twenty minutes, but he left. I felt disgusting. I wanted a shower and a change of clothes, but I didn't leave Jonathan's bedside. I didn't call anyone. Jonathan was burned badly. His face was covered in blisters and boils. I felt it was best if I handled it alone.

After that, I spent my time caring for Jonathan's burn. I made sure his bandage was changed every day and his creams were applied correctly. If I could do nothing more, at least I could care for him until he was better.

*   *   *

After a night of pizza and video games, I was tired. I changed Jonathan's bandages and put him to bed.

I lay in bed thinking about how difficult my life had become.

Yet, I was thankful because Jonathan's burns could have been worse. The doctor said his face would heal, even though his chest would have a scar. I was glad that the scar would be on his chest and not his face.

Two weeks after I returned from Kalamazoo, on May 14, I began to feel restless. I needed to leave the house. I decided to get a pedicure. Jonathan was feeling self conscious about his face.

"Do you want to go over to Grandma Walter's house while I get my toes done?" I asked him while driving to Lee Nails.

He nodded his head yes, and I headed toward the West side.

Driving down Hollyway Street, I noticed an ambulance in the distance. The ambulance was parked outside someone's house, and its lights were flashing. Mom lived on Hollyway Street.

I realized that the ambulance was on my block. Then suddenly it dawned on me that the emergency vehicle was in front of my mom's house. I breathed in sharply. *Whats going on?*

I pulled up and got out my car. Before I could ask a question, Uncle Mitch, my mom's older brother, came to the porch. "Your mom's in the ambulance. Ride with her," he told me.

I didn't know what to think, but I was relieved that Uncle Mitch was there and caring for my mom.

I walked to the back of the ambulance and knocked on the door. "That's my mom," I told the driver.

"I'm okay," Mom said, as she lifted her head off the gurney.

"Can you ride to the hospital with her?" the driver asked me.

I agreed. Uncle Mitch offered to let Jonathan stay with him while I rode to the hospital with my mom. I didn't think it was appropriate to bring Jonathan along in the ambulance so I let him stay with Uncle Mitch. Jonathan didn't protest. I'd grown up with Uncle Mitch so I trusted him with my son.

Later on, my dad brought Jonathan to the hospital with me and I took him home when I left.

Since I rode with Mom to the hospital, I was the one who handled all the family calls. And there were many. Word made it around my mom's family that she was in the hospital, and soon I began getting calls from cousins wanting to know if she was okay.

After a few hours, I decided to go for a walk around the hospital. I was tired of sitting in the ER. I spotted Yellow making her way to the entrance. I watched her walk through the revolving door. She had a wild look in her eyes as she searched around.

Look at Yellow lookin' crazy. Her eyes look like they about to pop out her head she's so scared. I almost laughed to myself.

I approached Yellow from behind. She was looking in all directions, trying to figure out where to go. Then she spotted me. She seemed relieved.

"She's fine," I said once I got close enough to my sister for her to hear.

"What happened?"

"I don't know. She can't move the left side of her body."

I led Yellow back to the ER, where Mom was resting.

We sat in the ER room for hours trying to decide what was going on.

Mom stayed in the hospital three days before she was released. No one wanted to take Mom in after she was released from the hospital. I decided to let her come to my house, even though I was leaving in less than a month.

I loved my mom. If I could have done more for her I would had. But I was given so few opportunities in life that I wasn't in the position to take care of her. I offered to help because I thought that my brothers, Yellow, and my dad would share the responsibility of Mom once she was released from the hospital. That didn't happen.

No one wanted to help me take care of Mom. She needed to be cooked for, bathed, dressed, and looked after. With caring for Jonathan's burn and taking him back and forth to the burn unit, I was overwrought.

After a week of trying to do it all myself, I spoke up and made my frustration known to my family. Soon fighting started. I saw a new side to my family.

Some people believe you can make a strong muscle weak by burdening it with extra weight. What they don't realize is that extra weight may, at first, cause the muscles to become sore and tender, but over time it makes the body stronger and speeds up the metabolism.

That's how it was for me. The first few weeks of my dilemma I was at the mercy of the forces of life, and then I began to build up my resistance.

The silly, catty games that my brothers and sisters played with me didn't discourage me. Rather, their games encouraged me, showing me that the time had come for me to move on from the family and the problems that came along with the family.

The games started when my brother, Earnest, didn't want to help me take Mom to her doctor appointment, even though he lived in her house and drove her car every day. From there, it progressed. Mom suggested that I put off my college plans and stay in Lansing to take care of her.

By two weeks from my move date, I was sick of everyone and ready to go. But there was one thing left to do—say good-bye.

*   *   *

The last few weeks in Lansing were the craziest for me. I began running into people that I hadn't seen in years. I took this as a sign that it was time to go. This was a chance for me to close open chapters in my life so I could move on.

The chance meeting that affected me most profoundly was with my old cosmetology teacher Ms. Marsha. Ms. Marsha was a soft-spoken black woman. She was small in stature and authority. Her appearance was plain, and beyond her weekly press and curl, she did little to enhance herself.

I ran into Ms. Marsha at Kroger the last week in May. We

spotted each other at the same time as I turned into aisle five to grab a box of Fruity Pebbles.

"Hey, Ms. Marsha," I said, excited to see my old teacher again.

Ms. Marsha looked the same. She wore large glasses over her small, round nose. Her skin was smooth and brown, and she wore a press and curl with a part on the side. She hadn't aged one day in the seven years since we'd last seen each other at the cosmetology good-bye dinner.

All the girls from the class had gotten together on the last day of school for lunch at Cheddar's. We decided to put our differences aside and go out to eat because we knew it would be the last time we'd be together, and we wanted to end the experience right. At the end of dinner, most of the girls were crying and hugging. I wasn't sad, and I didn't give anyone a hug. I knew I would see most of them around town, and I didn't care if I didn't.

We exchanged greetings and Ms. Marsha congratulated me on my acceptance at Western. I made it a point to let her know I was going off to college since all she remembered of me was being a single teenage mom in cosmetology class.

When I asked her what she had been up to, her answer set off an old issue.

"The same old thing—teaching at the school. I'm getting ready to take the girls to Chicago for the hair show in the spring."

In an instant I was angry. In the three years I was in cosmetology class no one had taken us to the hair show. Every year it was promised but for some reason put off. Ms. Marsha was my cosmetology teacher for my senior year; it was up to her to take us. She'd hinted at it but never got around to doing so.

Devastated, I looked at Ms. Marsha. My eyes grew wide. I opened my mouth in disbelief. "Ms. Marsha, why didn't you take us to the hair show?" I asked.

"Because you girls were awful. You were my worst class ever.

You girls never listened. I couldn't take you anywhere with me. You wouldn't behave."

Not believing that I was included in her insult, I asked, "Even me, Ms. Marsha?"

Ms. Marsha looked at me and, with a peaceful expression on her face, said, "You were the worst one."

I was offended at her comment. Ms. Marsha was a weak teacher. She let the class do whatever we wanted. My entire senior year I wasn't speaking to the other girls in the class because they had stopped talking to me and not once did Ms. Marsha try to interviene.

I was not the worst one in my class. I stayed to myself. The only times I engaged in an argument with any of the girls was when they had problems with me. Sometimes I didn't clean up when she asked or turn in my assignaments when she wanted but neither did any of the other girls. In my opinion she was just jealous.

I looked Ms. Marsha in the eyes and, in a soft voice, asked, "Ms. Marsha, are you serious? I couldn't have been the worst one. Those girls were loud, mean, and evil; they were a bunch of skanks."

She stared me directly in the eyes. In a slow, relaxed tone, she said, "You were the worst one."

I took a deep breath. Ms. Marsha wasn't angry, and she wasn't being nice either. I realized that this was a moment Ms. Marsha had been waiting for. When I was her student, she never could have told me the way she felt. Now was her chance.

I let her have her moment. We misbehaved in her class. I never listened to her. I did my own thing, even though I knew it got on her nerves. Because I wouldn't listen, none of the others girls would either.

"All right, Ms. Marsha," I said, looking sad.

She smiled and nodded. "I gotta go," she said.

"Okay. It was nice to see you," I told her.

"It was nice to see you too."

I watched Ms. Marsha walk away, swaying her hips as she made her way down the aisle.

I'd always wanted to run into some of my old teachers. Now I don't. I hope to avoid them from now on. I wonder how many of them feel that way about me now?

CHAPTER EIGHT:
Welcome to College

I MADE IT TO Kalamazoo with the help of Ryan, a friend I'd just met, Billy (Ryan's Friend), my brother Earnest and Earnest's best friend, Ben.

Jonathan, Ryan, Earnest and Ben, Billy and I, packed the truck all day on June 14 and left for Kalamazoo early the next morning.

Ryan was a medium height, medium build, brown-skinned man in his early twenties from Detroit. I'd met Ryan at a gas station a week before. I didn't know him that well, and we'd barely hit it off, but he had agreed to help me move free of charge, and Ryan even brought an extra helper—his friend Ben.

Billy was skinny with dark brown skin and hair. He didn't say much for the most part he packed in silence. Sometimes he exchanged conversation with Ryan and they joked with my brother earnest and Ben some. Overall the packing went smoothly and we were done in no time.

I was thankful for Ryan and Billy although I still didn't understand why he was so quick to help me free of charge.

Later on, I would understand his generosity. Ryan and I had no chemistry, and every time I tried to cut him off and tell him my feelings, he reminded me that he had helped me move to Kalamazoo. He even would go so far as to complain about backaches, hoping to induce spasms of guilt in me. By this time I was in kalamazoo and busy with college. I grew tired of his games and our friendship ended less than a month after I moved.

I was beginning to understand what it meant to take favors from people. They usually wanted something in return, even if was just the right to be annoying.

The drive to Kalamazoo took a little over two hours because Earnest, who was driving the U-Haul, had to drive slowly. I stayed beind the U-Haul truck which Ryan drove with Billy sitting beside him. I stayed in front of earnest because he didn't know the way. I tried to ignore Earnest when he called my cell phone to complain that I was switching lanes too often.

We arrived at campus full of energy. I will still in shock over the fact that I had actually made it.

Sometimes reality could feel like a daydream. I floated through campus, my mind drifting from one thought to the next without so much as a reaction. It was all new to me. A novice explorer, I followed behind the U-Haul in a trance.

I still had to sign my lease and pick up my keys before we could unload the truck. I found the student services building located across campus. The lease signing was simple and quick. My lease was only extended for one semester at a time, and there was no credit check.

It wasn't until I opened the door to my campus apartment that the rush of emotion hit me. I stared around the small, two-bedroom apartment in astonishment. The entire apartment was smaller than the main floor at my condo. The walls were cement bricks, the floor a thin layer of padding-free carpet. The kitchen was small with a stove so small that only the burners fit. A small window in the kitchen overlooked a large grass area with picnic tables.

Thoughts poured through my head. *I can't believe this apartment; it's so ugly,* I thought. *This is the worst apartment I've ever lived in. Everything is brown and yellow. The carpet is brown; the cabinets are brown; even the white venetian blinds have turned brown. The bathrooms are small, but at least it's decent. My room is small as hell. Jonathan's room is straight. It's about the same size as before. I'm so glad I got rid of all my shit, but I don't think this is gonna be enough room for what I brought. Damn.*

Not knowing what else to do, I filled a bucket with water, added Pine-Sol, and began washing the cabinets.

Ryan came into the apartment. "You cleaning up?" he asked.

"Yeah. I'ma start cleaning the cabinets."

"You tryin' ta get started already?"

"Uh-huh. I got a lot of unpacking to do. I'ma clean up and start unpacking the kitchen while you guys unload the truck."

And that's what I did. Earnest was supportive when he saw the apartment. "It's small, but you're in college," he told me.

He was right. I smiled as I looked around, realizing that my dream had come true. Jonathan was fairly quiet as he looked around his room. I could tell he didn't like it, but it was a sacrifice we had to make.

I'd known when I'd had him at sixteen that the road would be rough. I'd started out with nothing, and eight years later, I still lacked the necessary skills to advance through life. I saw my degree not just as personal advancement but as an accomplishment for the family I'd created.

After the truck was unloaded, we went downtown to eat and get a feel for the city. The restaurant we tried was on the corner of Michigan and Portage Road. The Olde Peninsula had a brewery inside the restaurant and served a large variety of beers. The people at Olde Peninsula were nice.

I needed to drop the U-Haul off after we ate. I was able to get directions to a U-Haul in Kalamazoo and a map of the city from our waitress.

"This place is nice," Earnest said. "They give you everything here. They even give you a map."

We laughed and agreed.

After we ate, we headed over to U-Haul. I gassed the U-Haul and dropped it back off. I was ready to go back home and unpack. My moving crew loaded into my mom's car and left.

I returned home to my new life on campus.

The small apartment was filled with boxes—so many that we couldn't walk through the apartment. I had no couch and no dining room table; the only furnishings I'd brought were my bedroom sets and my wall decorations. I'd even gotten rid of my fifty-two-inch Sony widescreen television and my washer and dryer; I sold them to my dad for a low price, along with the sectional I'd had in the basement. None of my furniture was older than two years. I missed my things.

Jonathan still didn't say much as he looked around.

"Well ... this is our new home," I prompted.

I could tell that he didn't like it, but he was happy that I'd brought the cat with us. Jonathan busied himself by playing with Pepper as I unpacked the kitchen.

I awoke early the next morning before Jonathan and went for a walk around campus. Campus was beautiful. Strange bushes and flowers, rolling fields, trees, statues, and benches were sprinkled in among the large brick buildings. The newer buildings were mainly glass and had a modern feel. One section was blocked off for renovations; I walked around the yellow-taped area. After exploring the main strip on campus, I made my way toward the pond.

This is so beautiful and peaceful. Look at the ducks walking around.

For the next week, I stayed in the house unpacking and trying to make space. I was bored, but it didn't last. On the third day, I met a friend.

Jonathan and I were on our way home from a walk around campus.

"You'll like it here," I told him. "I'ma enroll you in school down here. So while I'm at school, you'll be at school."

"Will I still get to see the family?"

Fuck the family. Them bitches left me high and dry. I still ain't over the way I got played after Mom's stroke.

I knew I had to choose my words carefully. "Yes, you'll still get to see the family. You'll see them when we go to Lansing to visit."

We passed the track and then the student recreation center. We rounded the corner and then passed French Hall. Next to

French Hall were the Elmwood student apartments. We lived in D building. Soon after we passed the A building, a rust-colored, two-door compact car pulled up. A dark-skinned boy got out. "Hi," he said.

"Hi," I responded.

The boy approached. He had a large, round nose and even larger lips. His eyes were small and beady. He was short and on the small side.

"Hi, my name is Raheem," he said.

Raheem told me that he was from Detroit and was now a junior at Western. He stayed in Kalamazoo all year round, but most of the students returned home for the summer.

There was something special about Raheem. I could tell. He was different from most of the people I knew. We began hanging out every day; it turned out that Raheem knew all the black people on campus. He introduced me to all his friends. Raheem made sure I was never lonely. He was always there for me to talk to, and he listened closely when I told him about my life.

Despite the fact that I had left Lansing, I still had obligations there, and I knew it. I'd left behind a crippled mother and a plethora of unfinished business. I made it a point to return to Lansing as much as I could handle. I still needed closure.

During my first few months in Kalamazoo, I went to visit Mom almost every weekend. She was staying at the rehabilitation center at Ingham Regional Medical, the hospital where I'd had my shoulder surgery.

I was glad to see my mom at Ingham. There she was fed and bathed. They even had a special wash station so that she could get her hair washed. Mom was glad about that, and she had me braid her hair whenever I came to visit her at Ingham.

"I like it here. You can get special treatment," I told Mom, as I brushed through her long thick hair. She had been at Ingham for three weeks.

"I know. I'm getting better already," Mom said. "I can move my fingers."

I watched as she slowing moved her index and middle fingers back and forth. I smiled and said, "You're getting better by the day."

It hurt to watch my Mom's sagging body droop in her wheel chair. I still couldn't understand what had happened. She said that she had ridden my dad's bike around the corner, and when she got off, she couldn't feel the left side of her body.

I braided mom's hair as we talked. We talked about Dad and the fact that he had changed so drastically. Neither one of us liked him anymore. Dad acted as if he no longer liked mom. Dad used to go over to her house every day. Sometimes they would go out on dates. Now he didn't want to be bothered.

"I'm the ex-husband," Dad had told me when I questioned him about helping Mom. "This isn't my responsibility. I have my own life. I'm not gonna spend it taking care of my ex-wife."

This conversation changed the way I viewed my situation. Whose responsibility was Mom? Even as an ex-wife, she was still a valuable member of the family. My dad's attitude toward my mom's stroke would, over time, ricochet and be the cause for our divide.

Mom, Jonathan, and I stayed in the large visiting room with the shelf full of children's book and a nineteen-inch color TV hanging on the wall. The other patients were in their rooms, and so we had some privacy. I remained silent as I finished braiding Mom's hair. I needed to hurry. It was getting late, and I still had to drive back to Kalamazoo.

Mom was moved to a nursing home on July 17. I didn't like her being at the nursing home. She seemed too close to death. "You gotta get outta here," I told Mom. "You're only forty-eight. You're not ready to be in a nursing home. You gotta fight to get better. Work on your exercises day and night. You have to take your rehabilitation seriously."

Mom and I looked around at the old and the disabled. "I know," she said. "I don't want to be here. I want to go home. But

I have no one to take care of me when I go home. I can't cook or clean."

Listening to her talk, I began to hate everyone in the family. Earnest still lived with Mom, but he didn't want to be bothered. My dad, my cousin Sharay (Mom's niece), Yellow, and my grandma all lived within a five-minute walk from Mom's house, and yet, she had no one to help her. I vowed that if I ever got the money, I would hire someone to come in and cook and clean for her.

There was other unfinished business in my life—my son's father. Grey came to see me in Kalamazoo. He was moving out of state and wanted to say good-bye. I showed him my apartment, and we talked one last time.

Grey and I absorbed the view. I took in the way the tall grass swayed in the wind, the way the overgrown vines strangled each other as they raced to the tops of skimpy trees. I watched the leaves fan the branches, trying to cool them off as they fluttered in the wind. I listened to the quiet of the empty parking lot. I focused on the birds chirping in the distance. I noticed the way the sun reflected off the marshy water in the swamp.

It was my view. It was the view that I had given up my life in Lansing for. Regardless of the way I felt, I had no regrets. There were times when I was regretful about moving my son to a new new city where I didn't have any help. I knew that he missed our condo as much as I did. Moments passed in which I felt like a fool for following my dreams. Even though I wanted to be a college student fact was I was a sinlge mother with no support system in a new city where I knew no one. My life was hanging by a thread and I knew it.

Focus on what's in front of you. This is your new life. The condo days are over. Welcome to college.

CHAPTER NINE:
Report to Work Monday

FALL SEMESTER STARTED IN September, and Western Michigan University came alive. Thousands and thousands of students, teachers, faculty, and staff hurried to and fro. I hurried along with them, trying not to look lost as I dashed from one end of the campus to the other, looking for my lecture halls.

I had struggled through my summer classes. Computers were beyond hard and it had taken help from my classmates and the professor to pass with a C. The other class I'd taken was a fitness class, and I'd received and A, even though it was a lot of work. I took aerobics because I thought it would be an easy grade. After the third test and weekly chapter assignment, I knew I had to work.

I was glad that I had come to Western in the summer instead of starting in the fall. Both classes I took in Summer II went towards my required area courses. After the summer semester ended, I pulled out my checklist and marked off two more classes. My transfer classes from LCC had taken care of some of the required classes.

I remained conscious of my grades because I hadn't forgotten the promise I'd made to myself at my LCC graduation. I would graduate with a 3.0 or better. I knew I would.

I decided to take four classes during fall semester. I wanted to study human resource management. My plan was to plow through the required prerequisites then enter the business college.

Despite everything that had happened to me over the summer, I wanted to have fun my first year in college. After the fall semester, Raheem was officially the "it" guy on campus. He was president of the NAACP and had been elected the *black* homecoming king (there was also a white homecoming king and queen for the white students on campus).

I had always been interested in the NAACP and decided to join. Since Raheem was the president and my good friend I had no problem being accepted by the people.

The first meeting was held the second week of school. By the third meeting, I was voted secretary. I was beyond thrilled to get my nomination. I knew it was my friendship with Raheem that had gotten me my position. Because of him, I had high status among the crew.

I learned a lot from my year as secretary. For one, I realized that no one should get a position based solely on who he or she knows, yet popularity does bring in the crowd. The fact that everyone that was in position of power in our organization was also popular on campus kept our meetings full. Most times people came to the meetings just to see who was there and hoping that they might meet someone "cool."

If our meetings were empty of people Raheem, Brandon (the vice president), or any other board member would simply go out and invite their friends and they always came. In the end things got done and we were making progress.

Then issues over my appointment began to surface. Some felt that I didn't deserve my title and that I was only appointed because I was Raheem's friend. I would disagree. Those people were simply envious of my personal friendship with Raheem and let that rule their judgment. I was the secretary and I did whatever was asked of me. I smiled when I met important people and I took good notes.

But the problem was that our organization was unorganized. The Kalamazoo branch of the NAACP did nothing to guide us along, and although we made ample effort to make a difference, without guidance from the older generation, we were left unsure of how to do so.

It seemed that was the plague affecting the younger generation of the day. As much as we tried to change the world, those who ran it refused to give us support or pass on any know-how, and so decade after decade, things stay the same. If one is to make a change, he or she must receive knowledge from those who forged the way. Without the know-how accumulated over generations, the world would simply collapse.

Little by little, I was beginning to understand Raheem. But it wasn't until homecoming weekend on October 15 that I got it fully.

I wasn't expecting to go to the October 15 step show. Jonathan and I were walking around campus on one of our daily walks. I had on a pair of dingy sweat pants, an old T-shirt, and gym shoes. Jonathan wore a pair of old blue jeans, a T-shirt and gym shoes as well. After we passed the large water fountain by Miller Auditorium, we noticed a large crowd of dressed up black people.

"What's going on down there?" Jonathan asked.

"I don't know. Come on. Let's go find out."

We wiggled our way through the large crowd. I spotted Brent, a friend of Raheem's, standing by the doorway. We waved at each other. I made my way over toward him.

"What's going on?" I asked.

"The step show. They also gonna announce the black homecoming king and queen."

It had slipped my mind that it was homecoming weekend. The vote had already taken place the day before in the Bronco Mall. Raheem was on the ballad. Homecoming was all the students talked about, but I had forgotten. The only time I paid attention to campus life was when I was on campus. Being in the apartment didn't count.

"Wanna stay and watch the step show?" I asked Jonathan.

"Sure."

I followed Brandon upstairs to where his crew was located. I spotted Raheem talking to a few girls. He left them and came over to give me a hug.

"What's up, Jonathan?" Raheem asked, giving Jonathan a pound.

I could tell Jonathan felt cool being a part of the college in crowd. He tried to look nonchalant as he surveyed the crowd. Hundreds of people milled about; some looked frantic, and others seemed lost.

Raheem and his crew looked in charge. They stood around, dominant, waiting to be approached. I found a bench close to them and sat down. One by one, they made their way over to say hello. I only knew Raheem's closest friends; the others simply stood back and asked about me.

I noticed Brandon quietly watched the other girls. They tried to get his attention, waving and giggling at him. Brandon looked them over. The girls were fresh out of high school—skinny bodies, tight clothes, fresh perms, new acrylic nails, bright makeup. Then Brandon glanced at me.

I sat quietly on the bench away from the crowd, keeping an eye on Jonathan as he ran around. I was dressed to lounge, not caring about my appearance. I had a blank expression as I watched the girls sashay around gaining attention from the boys. I was twenty-five, and I had the stresses of a twenty-five-year-old.

I've already done this in Lansing, I thought to myself. I remembered the icebreakers and the step shows out at MSU. Even though was here, I wasn't a part of that. I was too old.

And it was the truth. I had my son with me, and he was not interested in the step show. Although I was a college student, I was still a mom, and to me that was the most important thing.

I smiled at Brandon as he made his way over to me. He shooed several girls away. "Hey, Nova, how's it going?" he asked.

"Good."

"You havin' a good time?"

"Yeah. There's a lot of people here."

"Come sit in the balcony with us."

Raheem and his crew had an entire section reserved in the right side balcony. I felt protected being with them.

The step show was interesting. Different fraternities and sororities showcased their talents. Spinning, clapping, stomping, stepping in unison, they were the symbol of black mobility.

Jonathan was bored with the step show, and so was I. I promised him that we would leave as soon as the homecoming results were announced.

I watched the Sigmas walk across the stage, followed by a few other sororities and fraternities. Finally it was time for the king and queen to be announced. The results were in. Raheem had won. Along with the thousands of other students, I screamed and applauded for Raheem.

Raheem stepped on stage. He took the microphone from the host. He looked at the crowd, serious and devoted, and said, "Detroit, stand up."

Even though I wasn't from Detroit, I wanted to stand and applause with the roar of the crowd. The Detroit people jumped to their feet, proud to have one of their own crowned.

Raheem gave his thank you speech. I was as happy for him as he was for himself as I watched him humbly accept his honor. "Thank you," Raheem said.

"I really appreciate this. I want to thank everyone who voted for me."

He's a special person. People love him, I thought. *Raheem is the most loved person on campus. They do whatever he says. That boy is somethin' else.*

"Let's go," I said to Jonathan as soon as Raheem left the stage.

We hurried down the stairway. The carpeted stares absorbed the sound of our footsteps as we made our exit. On my way out the door, I spotted Raheem. We hugged each other.

"Congratulations," I said. "I'm so happy for you."

"Thanks. Where're you going?"

"Home. I wanted to stay to watch you win."

Raheem and I smiled at each other. I felt special knowing that I was one of his friends.

"This is such a wonderful moment. It's so amazing that you got to be homecoming king." I told him smiling.

"And you're the first person I got to see."

Raheem looked me hard in the eyes. We stared at each other. I smiled at Raheem. There was warmth between us that couldn't be explained. I didn't like him as a boyfriend. He already had a girlfriend. It had taken me months to find out about her, and he hadn't told me about her himself, but nonetheless, she was there.

Raheem and I were complete opposites. He was five years younger than me. He was super popular, and I was a nerd. He'd played baseball in high school while I'd had a baby. He hung out with his friends on the weekends while I stayed home with my son. And yet, we had chemistry. College put us on the same level in a lot of ways.

The homecoming queen came down the stairs. A pretty, light-skinned girl with soft, shoulder-length hair, she stood back waiting on Raheem. They had to make an appearance together.

"I gotta go," he said.

"All right, call me later." I turned to the girl. "Congratulations," I said.

She smiled at me. I glanced over at Raheem. He gave me a warm smile. I knew how to play the game. He didn't like jealous girls; no man did.

For the next few weeks, I enjoyed school. I went to play bingo with Alyson, a girl I'd met during summer school, and went for walks around campus. I hung out with Raheem and his crew. Sometimes I even forgot about Grey.

Life was going well for me, until things took an unexpected turn. My restriction for no work at or above should lever ran out on Monday, October 31. Without new restrictions, I was to go back to the line immediately.

In addition to my restriction ending, Workers Compensation sent me notification that I had a doctor's appoint in Jackson, Michigan, on October 26. I wasn't expecting Workers Comp to step in.

For the last two years, GM had handled all my medical care exclusively. I saw nothing but GM doctors and went to physical therapy at the GM Fisher Body plant. I didn't know what to expect from Workers Comp.

It rained on the day I went to see Dr. Tillman in Jackson. I downloaded directions to his office from MapQuest; however, the directions did not take into account the road construction taking place throughout the city. Because of this, I was almost twenty minutes late for my appointment.

I drove through downtown Jackson, careful not to hit one of the large potholes dotting the streets as I searched for a parking spot. Each passing second catapulted me closer to panic.

Damn I didn't want to be late for this appointment. I hope this doesn't hurt my exam, I thought as I rushed through the double doors of Southworth Medical Center.

I headed toward the elevator and then on to the second floor.

"Hi, my name is Nova Wallace. I have a ten thirty appointment with Dr. Tillman," I said to the receptionist.

"You're twenty minutes late."

I stared at her round face, focusing in on the green of her eyes behind her thick glasses and said, "I know. My directions got me lost on the way in. I didn't expect the road construction."

She gave me a subtle eye roll. "I'll go talk to the doctor. It's up to him whether he'll see you or not."

"Okay," I said, patiently.

I hope this ain't gonna be no bullshit. I had already driven an hour to get there and since I wasn't the one that made the appointment I knew there would be issues with rescheduling. I was nervous that I had arrived too late. Then the receptionist called me back up to the window.

"He says he'll still see you," she said.

Relieved I took me seat again. I looked around the waiting room, noticing the other patients.

Damn, they all look like dirty factory workers. Everyone smells like oil. They all have on combat boots and jeans. I'm sitting here in a satin top, flashy blazer, makeup, and a fresh hairdo. I'm overdressed. Fuck.

Dr. Tillman, a tall, blond, white man with a thick mustache stared at me with cold blue eyes and asked, "How did you injure you shoulders?"

"I had a job that required me to work over my head. I had to reach up and attach the hoses to the cars. It was all the overhead pushing and pulling that did it."

"Do you have mobility in your shoulders now?"

"Yes. I can reach above my head. It's just that, when I do, there's a lot of pain."

"Describe the pain."

"It's a dull, burning feeling. Sometimes there is a sharp pain. My shoulders feel sore and swollen all the time."

"Is the pain in both shoulders?"

"Yes. But it hurts more on the left. I had surgery on the left to stop it from snapping, but sometimes it still snaps."

"Do you take anything for pain?"

"Not right now. Sometimes I take extra-strength Vicodin. But I'm out right now."

I sat on the examination table fully dressed in my street clothes. *Damn, why so many questions*, I thought. *Why aren't you examining me.*

I was annoyed by the way he was treating me. He acted as a company lawyer instead of a doctor. I had real questions that needed direct answers. I didn't look at our meeting as a Workers compensation meeting, I viewed this as a chance to discuss my injury with a specialist and I wanted to be treated as so.

Dr. Tillman continued his questioning. "What tasks can you perform?" he asked, his stare becoming colder, his disposition watchful and suspicious.

"I can cook, clean, do my hair, get myself dressed. I also take care of my son."

Dr. Tillman continued with his questioning. Then he had me get up from the examination table. "Lift your hands over your head."

I complied.

"Good. Now bend over and touch your toes."

Bend over and touch my toes? I ain't never had a doctor ask me that. Damn, he gonna be lookin all down my shirt. But fuck it.

I had already removed the blazer that I was wearing, exposing my low-cut, V-neck top. My 36 DD breast busted out the top of my blouse when I bent over to touch my toes.

Dr. Tillman leaned over and stared down my shirt as I bent over and touched my toes. "All right, your exam is over," he said. "I'll send the results over to General Motors."

"Okay," I responded, adding, "I have a question. What are the chances that I will develop arthritis in my shoulders?"

"Very slim. The spot where the bone is scraped is not a place where arthritis usually sets in." Then he looked at me and, in a serious tone, said, "Your injury is one that people usually recover from."

I was glad to hear that I would heal. Dr. Tillman's words gave me hope that one day I would make a full recovery.

Despite the pain and soreness in my shoulders, I had to report to work as requested. I was sad that I couldn't spend Halloween with Jonathan. I drove him to Lansing and prepared to go to work that night. Mom had been released from the nursing home and was back home.

For sixty-five dollars a week, Mom agreed to be my babysitter. I would have called my old babysitters, Doc and Mrs. Janice, who normally kept Jonathan while I worked, but since I was unsure if my return was permanent, I let Mom watch him. She needed the money.

I spent eighty dollars on Jonathan's Halloween costume that year. He was a monster with a large knife and a scary mask. I always spent big on Jonathan when I worked. I made up for the fact that we never saw each other when I worked the night shift with expensive gifts.

Returning to work had seemed surreal, until I parked my car in the parking lot at the Lansing Grand River Plant. Only then did I realize how hugely the return would impact my life.

Behind me, I could hear the gurgle of the Grand River as I locked my car door and began the nearly ten-minute walk from my car to the into plant.

Before I could return to work on the line, I had to go to medical for clearance. The medical department had been moved to the training center. The training center stood just outside the main gate of Lansing Grand River.

I walked into a small lobby area and made my way to the security desk. "I have an appointment with medical," I told the security guard.

She buzzed me in with no problems. I walked through the large, glass double doors and walked along the carpeted hallway to the plant's medical department.

My appointment was with Dr. Washington. I had never met Dr. Washington before. He was the head doctor for GM in Lansing. I had received no word from the Workers Compensation about my evaluation. I knew that whatever Dr. Tillman had written in his report would greatly impact Dr. Washington's decision.

I stared at Dr. Washington. He watched me from behind his glasses, sizing me up, deciding. My file was in front of him. He read it in silence.

"Have you worked since your injury?" he asked me.

"No."

"How are you feeling now?"

"I am still in a lot of pain. Sometimes my left shoulder snaps."

"Have you been examined by any other doctors since you last saw Dr. Wells?"

"Yes, Workers Comp sent me to a doctor a few days ago."

Dr. Washington frowned; deep crinkles appeared in his pale forehead. "I don't have that report here. Hold on. Let me go find out where it is."

Dr. Washington left me alone.

I hopped this was good news. I was still in a lot of pain. *God, please don't let them send me back,* I pleaded silently.

My prayer went unanswered. Dr. Tillman had diagnosed me as able to return to work. "That is what Workers Comp ruled," Dr. Washington said. "I'm going to agree with their decision. I'm returning you to work with no restrictions."

What! Did you hear me when I said my shoulder hurt? How the fuck am I supposed to survive on the line with no damn restrictions? It's fucked up enough that you're sending me back, but with no restrictions—that's bullshit.

"I'm not ready to go back to work," I said, pissed off. "I've already told you my shoulders hurt. I'm not gonna let you cripple me."

Dr. Washington sucked in his breath, opening his eyes wide. He motioned for the nurse to come in the room. When she did, he said, "Prepare a return to work interview." He turned to me. "Go with her. She has some questions for you. She'll enter it into the computer. If you don't feel that you're ready to return to work, then say that in your interview." He looked at me sternly. "GM is no longer handling your case. We have done all that we can for you. From now on, if you want to stop working, you'll have to have your primary care doctor take you out."

"So I'm supposed to go out there and work with no restrictions?" I said, as I followed Dr. Washington back to the front desk.

"Yes. We're not trying to ..." he paused and looked at me. "What is that word you used?"

"Cripple—I said you were trying to cripple me."

Dr. Washington gave the nurse a look. "Yes, cripple. We're not trying to cripple you. GM has done all it can. You must go to your family doctor."

With that, Dr. Washington went to the back room to look at another patient.

"This isn't over. You're gonna see me again. And again. And again. And again," I called out after him.

Dr. Washington let out an amused laugh and walked into an exam room.

After I finished the return interview with the nurse, I took my return slip out of the nurse's hand and silently left the medical department. I walked over to the paint department to find a supervisor and get placed on a job.

I recognized a few faces as I entered the main doors at the paint department. I didn't remember my coworkers well enough to say hi, and no one spoke to me as I headed upstairs to the offices.

There were many offices at LGR. I headed to the main office overlooking the assembly line. This was where the offices of the immediate supervisors and the man Power coordinator were located.

A large white man with a balding head and glasses stood at a desk looking at a computer screen. I walked over to him and said, "Hi, I just returned to work today. I'm not sure where I'm supposed to go."

Any supervisor in the main office could figure out what I needed to do. If he or she didn't know, finding out was as simple as getting on the walkie-talkie.

The balding man looked at me confused. "What's your name?" he asked.

"Nova Wallace."

"Where are you coming from?"

"Medical leave. I've been off for the last two years. I have a shoulder injury."

He looked frustrated. I read the name on the badge hanging from his collar: "Tim/Man Power Coordinator."

"I'm still in a lot of pain," I added. "Even though I don't have any restrictions, I can't work above my head."

I wanted to let him know where I stood. Even though I had been returned to work, I had no plans on staying.

Hearing this, Tim frowned. "We're completely full in the paint department. There are no jobs open. Where did you work?"

"I was the extra. I know how to do some of the jobs in foam department. I know how to do one of the jobs in primer. Most of the time I was here I was on restrictions, and so I did quality checks."

Tim went on to explain the situation to me. Medical had not informed him that I was coming. I wondered why, but I didn't press the issue. Perhaps Dr. Washington wanted to see if I would even show up for work.

Tim informed me that a few people had been tagged to go work in the body shop and another person was leaving to go to first shift in general assembly. I could take their jobs; however, there were people already waiting to get those jobs. If I bumped them, the union would get involved.

"Let me call the union rep. and see what he says. I'm pretty sure that you have the right to stay in the paint department. I'm not sure what we're gonna do yet. Most new people start in sealer, although you're not new," Tim said.

"Don't worry about trying to find me a job. I won't be here long. My shoulders still hurt."

I had already made an appointment to see my surgeon the next day. As soon as received the notification to return to work while in Kalamazoo I called Dr. Wells on my cell phone and made my appointment. I decided right then and there that I would put up a good fight.

Tim nodded in understanding. He looked like an experienced supervisor. That meant he understood what was going on. Most people who returned from long medical leaves didn't stay long. I didn't want to try and become a part of a group knowing I was leaving.

The union representative confirmed what Tim already knew. If he placed me on one of the open jobs, the people who were waiting to get those jobs could file a grievance. I agreed to go to the sealer line, even though that meant I had to use an air gun. All the jobs in sealer were overhead. That meant that I would have to hold a gun up over my head for at least eight hours a day. My shoulders began to hurt just from the thought.

Tim and I walked out of the soundproof office and onto the line. I remained silent as I followed behind him, remembering the last time I was on the line. I recognized a few faces, and a few of the workers recognized me. We exchanged smiles and waves as I followed Tim to the sealer line.

Tim introduced me to my supervisor—a young white woman with straight, brown, shoulder-length hair. She turned to me and introduced herself as Karen.

"Hi, my name is Nova."

We had to talk loudly to hear each other over the hum of the line. Conveyor belts, engines, air tools, fans, radios, and people yelling and laughing caused a continuous roar that echoed through the hollow building.

Karen introduced me to my team leader, a Hispanic woman named Maria. I already knew Maria from the south plant. I was happy to see that Maria had moved up to the rank of team coordinator. That meant she only had to be on the line when help was needed.

Maria was still pretty. Maria and I talked as we worked. She told me that she had been married and still had no children.

I did my job with no complaint, although I was in excruciating pain. I had to reach up and open the driver's side door, which had not been officially attached. The door was difficult to open. Once I got the door open, I had to squeeze a small amount of sealer onto designated seals.

There was one long seal along the bottom floor of the front of the car. The seal went up and above my head. After I did that, I had to grab a special metal door opener and place it in the front door to keep it open for the jobs down the line. Then I had to do a couple of seals in the back of the car and then place another door opener in the rear door.

The movements were smooth and timed. I had to work with my partner who stood across from me. We timed our movements. Within thirty minutes, my left shoulder was throbbing.

On break, I walked up the stairs to the team break room. I unzipped my blue paint suit and sat down at the break table. While I sat at the break table reading the newspaper, Greg, an old friend from the South plant, stopped to talk to me. We caught up on old times, and I told him about my injury.

"You remember Rosa?" he asked.

"Yeah, we hired in together."

"She's been out almost two years because of her injury," Greg told me. Then he lowered his voice and looked away. "But I don't think there's nothin' wrong with her."

I stared at Greg's bald head, fat stomach, brown skin, and pointed nose and tried not to show contempt for his comment. Years working at GM had shown me how the other line workers treated people who got injured. Maybe back in the day people faked injuries, but with the doctors and laws today, it was impossible to fake a comp case.

I finished out the rest of the night. I got off at two-thirty in the morning. Hurt and tired, I picked Jonathan up from Mom's house and started the nearly hour and a half drive back to Kalamazoo.

I went to see Dr. Wells in Okemos the next morning. We had a serious conversation about GM and what was to happen next. He was surprised to hear that my left shoulder still cracked.

"I shaved a lot of bone off. I don't see how it can still crack. There's not much left," he told me.

What the hell you mean you scraped a lot off? You hacked me up. That's probably why I'm still in pain.

"The cracking started up again last night. It was doing okay.

It hardly ever cracked. But now, they have me working over my head holding a gun. It's too much for me."

"I'll place you on restriction, but I'm going to tell you now, GM will not honor your restrictions. They don't have to."

"Okay, thanks. I'ma still try, though."

"Is there anything else you need?"

"No."

"Okay. Call me if you need me."

Dr. Wells was correct. I stopped by the medical department before I headed into work that night. Dr. Washington refused to honor my restrictions, and then he told me not to return to the medical department.

Later that night, I complained to Karen about shoulder pain, but she refused to let me go to medical. "Medical has informed me that they already know about your condition. They said they already told you what to do."

By the second day, Tuesday, the pain had begun to affect me. My mind began to reject what was happening to me. I stared down the line at the hundreds of cars on their way to my station. I looked up the line at the hundreds of cars that had already passed. I began to feel as if I wouldn't make it—as if I would have a nervous breakdown.

Wednesday I did a "no call, no show." I decided I wasn't going into work, and I didn't bother calling. The old me would have never dared do such a thing; now I couldn't care less.

I went into work on Thursday. "Why didn't you call?" Karen asked.

"To be honest, I'm in a lot of pain, and I didn't care to call. All I want to do is get out of here. I want to use a vacation day to make up for the pay."

Karen smiled at me and nodded her head. She understood. "Because you have a good work record, I'm just going to give you a verbal warning. Normally, I don't have to let you use a vacation day without an excuse. I'll do it this time," she said.

"Thank you."

What kept me going was Rosa. She had returned that Thursday after being away from the plant for nearly two years. Rosa wanted to work, although she was in great pain.

"I have three daughters who all have children and no man to help. I have to come here. I need the money," Rosa told me while we worked across from one another. "Before I was hired at GM, I worked nearly eighty hours a week to make the money I make here. Are you still in school?"

"Yeah, I go to Western. Right now I'm commuting back and forth."

"Good. Don't stop going to school. I have no education, so I have no choice. You're still young. Get an education so you can get out."

Rosa told me about her injury. She'd had two surgeries that summer. Since she was allergic to pain medication, she'd had to recover with nothing."

"Damn, Rosa. That's fucked up," I said. "You couldn't take nothin'? Wow. I know I need to take a Vicodin right now. My shoulders are killing me. I can't believe they sent me back to work with no restrictions."

"These doctors don't care. I had a doctor give me the okay to return to work. I walked out of her office and fainted as soon as I made it outside. Some people had to pick me up and carry me back inside. They got rid of her though. She was a bitch. I had to go to my doctor and have him take me out."

"Your doctor had you out all this time?"

"Yeah."

"And did you still get your Workers Comp checks?"

"Yeah."

Rosa went on to explain how it worked. I listened closely because I wasn't sure what to do. Even Dr. Washington had told me to go to my family doctor. I wasn't sure if I would still get the same amount of pay if my primary doctor took me out of work.

I'd had my doctor take me off of work for a stress relief period before, but the pay for that period was almost half of what I received with Workers Comp and disability. I thought that if I had my doctor take me off again, I would only get sick leave pay. Rosa explained that I would still be with Workers Comp, even though GM was no longer keeping me out.

Thanks, Rosa. You don't know how much your advice has changed my life, I thought as I listened to her.

I watched Rosa for the rest of the night. She sang and danced, moving her petite waist to the sound of her favorite Latin bands. Her butterscotch complexion glowed under the florescent lights. Her long hair pulled back into a ponytail bounced to the rhythm of her feet.

I watched her face, studied her eyes. Rosa did everything to mentally remove herself from the line.

I made an appointment with my family doctor. Dr. Moore wasn't in, so I saw another physician, Dr. Michaels. Dr. Michaels took me off work for a month. He told me to come back in a month to be reevaluated.

When the month was up, I went back to my doctor's. I'd made an appointment with Dr. Moore in advance. This time, I'd come prepared. I had researched my condition. I brought with me all the information I had saved from Dr. Wells plus the information I'd printed out on the Internet explaining my condition—snapping scapula syndrome.

Dr. Moore was impressed but not convinced. "Even with your condition, you can still work," he told me.

Dr. Moore sat across from me giving me a stern look. Dr. Moore was a white man with an average build, a potbelly, a moustache, and a neatly trimmed beard. I stared at the posters highlighting the details of different medical conditions that were tacked up around his office.

"I want to work. I'm going to school. I go to Western," I said. "I just can't do factory work."

Dr. Moore looked at me. "So that's why you moved to Kalamazoo. You go to Western." Then he understood.

I was glad he understood. I wasn't playing games or dodging

my responsibility at GM. I knew that my life with GM was over. I was making plans for my future.

Dr. Moore took me out of work permanently. I had him send me back to physical therapy to try and heal my shoulders. Workers Comp and disability picked me back up, and I continued my life in college.

I didn't do great that semester. I had to drop my two most difficult classes—economics and theater. I'd thought theater would be easy. Raheem had taken the class and said it was fun. Unfortunately for me, I never had a babysitter, and it was difficult for me to make it to all the required plays and shows.

I kept attending my other two classes. I finished organizational behavior with a C and marketing with a D/C.

Disappointed that my GPA had dropped, I remained positive by focusing on the fact that I had passed. I signed up for my classes for the spring semester and kept my momentum going.

Although I had solved my GM problem, another issue remained unresolved—my condo. I still had no buyer. I'd put my condo up for rent in September, but the management company had not found a renter. Unsatisfied with the service, I decided to drop Silverstone Management and take over as the landlord.

On my own, I had to find a renter and manage the property. I decided to drop the rental price from $980.00 a month to $750.00. On the day I decided this, Green called me.

Green had moved back from Nashville and was looking for an apartment. He asked to be my renter. I told him how much the rent was, and he agreed. On December 9, 2006, he moved in, along with two other roommates that he knew well.

I had many things going on at the time. Still healing from losing Grey, I had to continue to take care of Jonathan and focus on being a single mom. The holidays were approaching. My first six months in Kalamazoo proved brutal. But still, I was happy to be in college.

Chapter Ten:
Trouble with Topaz

There was another issue brewing in my life—Topaz. Even though there were problems with our friendship and we still weren't over the James incident we talked on the phone nearly every day. I wasn't mad at her for being the way she was. I accepted her attitude as a factor in our friendship.

Topaz had left Lansing to move to Pennsylvania in May 2005. I believe she left so she could be closer to James, who had been convicted in a drug case. In April 2005, he'd started serving time in a Pennsylvania penitentiary. It was strange saying good-bye to Topaz again.

When I was twenty-one, she'd moved to Warrington. She hadn't liked it there, and so she'd moved back to Lansing after a year in Warrington. Now Topaz was moving back to Pennsylvania and I didn't think she was going to like it this time around. Topaz claimed that she was moving to Pennsylvania for nursing school. She told me that the nursing programs in Pennsylvania were better than the ones in Michigan. In addition, she would finish her training in eighteen months—ironically, right around James's release date.

Topaz spent her first year in Pennsylvania visiting James and partying at the bar. Since she was in the bar almost every night, Topaz decided to get a job at the bar as a waitress. That's when she met Clark. After a few weeks, she was expecting a child.

"I'm pregnant, and I'm getting married," Topaz told me over the phone.

I was surprised, but since she sounded sure of her decision, I gave her my congratulations. It was May 2006, and Topaz had been gone a year. I was surprised at the news but not that much. Topaz was twenty-four at the time. She seemed ready for a baby.

Topaz visited Lansing that August. She was three months pregnant. I drove from Kalamazoo to see her. We hung out for the day, and she seemed happy. At three months pregnant, she was showing, but her bump was small and she still looked pretty. Topaz had a beautiful diamond ring on her finger and talked about her wedding plans.

By September 1 2006, she was no longer engaged.

"I'm sick of his bitch," Topaz told me during a phone conversation.

I was sittin in my room watching the leaves change colors in preparation for fall. Jonathan was in the living room playing video games. I was interested in what she had to say about Clark and so I listended closely.

"Last night, she came in the restaurant while me and Clark was eating, and the bitch threw a plate of food at me. Then she spit on me. I tried to get after her, but Clark jumped in between us... I don't know why she's still around. She sees me sitting there, pregnant, with an engagement ring on my finger. Why is the bitch trying ta' fight? I'm mad at Clark because he doesn't want to testify in court. He thinks this ain't got nothin' to do with him; it's our problem."

"What you mean it ain't got nothin' to do with him? It's his bitch," I said, pissed on her behalf.

Listening to the story about the restaurant made me recall another story Topaz had told me about Clark and his ex-girl friend. This had taken place about two weeks after she met him back in early April of 2006.

*   *   *

"I was lying in the bed asleep," she told me. "I woke up, and this bitch is standing over us. She climbed in the damn window ... She knows whenever he's at home or if I'm over because she lives in the building right in front of his apartment. The bitch doesn't have a job. She watches his apartment all day long."

I was shocked. It was the craziest thing I had ever heard of. I was scared for Topaz and wanted her to leave Clark alone.

"If the bitch ain't leaving him alone, it's for a reason," I advised. "Cut him off. She's crazy.Take it from me, you don't need a crazy bitch in your life. I don't understand why she don't just move on."

"Because this is a small ass town, and he's the best thing that ever happened to her," Topaz had explained.

*   *   *

Now, I listened as she ranted about what she would do to the girl for spitting on her.

I continued watching the leaves. We were like the leaves, Topaz and I. We were changing color. Still undecided as to what color we would be we hung on to our old tree, swallowing the last of the sun. I wondered when we would fall.

"Fuck it, just move on," I told her. "He must like her if he ain't doin' nothin' 'bout her tryin' to jump on you while you're pregnant."

For the most part, I listened quietly as she complained about the situation with Clark. I didn't feel like I was a part of her life anymore. Topaz fed me information about Clark with a long-handled spoon, and I let her. I didn't want to know.

During her pregnancy, all Topaz talked about was Clark's drug money—how much of it he spent on her. She talked about his Cadillac as if it was her own. To me, it sounded like bragging; but not being jealous, I let her brag. Even though she was no longer engaged, she still dated Clark. Sometimes Topaz wanted to call the wedding back on; sometimes she didn't.

By late September, Topaz was very nervous about her child's father selling drugs. She wanted him to give up the streets and move to Lansing with her. At first he refused, but as time went on, he was coming around.

Topaz went to Lansing and found and apartment for the two of them. She signed her lease on September 17.

Topaz was angry because Clark complained about giving her $2,500 for new furniture, yet he went to Vegas and blew $15,000. I knew it then—something was seriously wrong with Clark.

I began to suspect that Clark didn't care about Topaz, but she kept telling me stories about his money. She comforted me and herself by saying that he would give her more when he came back from Vegas. Clark had acted similarly about Topaz's wedding ring. He wasn't happy about spending $2,000 on a ring, when he spent more than that on a trip to the mall.

Topaz had her first ultrasound. It was then, in late September, that she learned the devastating news about her son. He had a large hole in his heart. Topaz was unsure about continuing on with the pregnancy but Clark was still around and he convinced her to carry on with the pregnancy. This was prior to Clark's arrest.

It would be some time before Topaz told me about her son's heart condition. Only after the devastation, disappointment, abandonment, isolation, fear, and self regret she faced, would she come clean about her situation. I didn't find out about her baby's condition until December. By then she had no choice but to continue on with the pregnancy. If I would have known sooner I would have talked her out of having a sick baby by a drug dealer. She didn't need that in her life.

By the beginning of October, Topaz had convinced Clark to move to Lansing. She had been in Lansing a couple of weeks by herself and had made it clear that she wasn't going back to Warrington. Realizing he would never see his child otherwise, Clark agreed to make the move.

Topaz went to Warrington to help Clark pack up his things. It was then that the FBI made its move. On October 29, federal agents busted Clark with ten keys of cocaine and $50,000 in cash. They froze all his bank accounts, including Topaz's. They even took her car until she showed check stubs to prove that she had the means to have paid for it. She was five months' pregnant.

Once things went south, Topaz began opening up about Clark. She told me he had already served ten years in prison before he met her. That surprised me.

"How long had he been out when you met him?" I asked.

"Three months," she said.

Three months? You got pregnant by a man you'd known for just a few weeks who'd only been out of prison for three months. He probably knew he was going back when he met you; that's why he's so thirsty for a kid. And that's why he was trickin' so hard. Damn.

I asked Topaz more questions about Clark. The more I found out, the more I thought Topaz had made a colossal mistake by failing to ask clark the same questions when she met him. "I don't ask questions," Topaz said sarcastically. "That's why they like me." She let out a sardonic chuckle.

I didn't say a word, and she grew quiet. She knew how I felt. I asked a question every other minute; that way I knew what was going on.

Well that's why you're in the situation you're in, no? I thought.

"That's probably why I haven't had much success with drug dealers," I told her. "I ask a lot of questions. I need to know what's going on. When's he getting out?"

Topaz let out a long sigh. "Probably never. They have a lot of evidence against him. His best friend snitched. I told him not to trust anyone. They've been friends since they were four years old."

"Damn," I said.

There was nothing that could be done. In the end, there was no money for a lawyer, and Clark was depending on a court-appointed attorney, the worst kind.

By December, when Clark had been locked up for almost a month, matters worsened for Topaz. James was released from prison in the beginning of December. James couldn't understand how Topaz couldn't wait eighteen months for him to get out. He wanted to see Topaz as soon as he was released, but I didn't think that was a good idea.

"Honestly, Topaz, you shouldn't go see James right now. The last time he saw you, you were skinny and had no kids. Now you're big and pregnant. He only wants to see you to be mean. Wait until you've had that baby and lost some weight before you go see him."

Topaz took my advice and only talked to James over the phone. Since James was staying at a halfway house in Grand Rapids, his time in Lansing was limited. James pressed Topaz every time he came to Lansing, but she was adamant about her refusal to see him, a decision she would be thankful for later. Topaz had gained nearly a hundred pounds during her pregnancy. She was not the same person. By December, she was swollen and looked puffy. I knew that James was still hurt about Clark. Even though he sounded happy for her, I knew that he would just dog her out.

*　　*　　*

Throughout November, December, and January Topaz had immersed herself in Clark's case, sending money and accepting phone calls. By February, she was tired of Clark and his court case. Plus, it was time for her baby to be born.

Topaz endured a long, painful labor. She stayed in active labor for nearly twenty-seven hours. She went into labor on Monday, February 7 and had her baby on February 8.

I called Topaz's phone early Tuesday morning to find out how she was. Her grandmother answered her cell phone. "She's hanging in there," she said. "The baby's in surgery right now. We're praying for him."

"I'll pray for him too," I said.

I'd known that Topaz's baby would need surgery even before he was born. I felt sorry for her when she told me but I was too busy with school and my new life to care that much. Every day from the time I moved to Kalamazoo we'd grown further and further apart. It was to the point that I barely answered her phone calls. I was having fun in college and I didn't want to hear about her baby issues.

Yet once the baby was born I was forced to come to terms with her situation and I found myself being sad and depressed. I came to realize that I did care for her and I loved her as my friend.

I prayed for the baby that day and again that night and once more in the morning. I didn't talk to Topaz during this time because she was in too much pain to talk.

I talked to Topaz that Thursday. Groggy, she told me that she was okay.

"I'm coming to see you Saturday," I said.

Because of the baby's heart condition, Topaz had her baby at the University of Michigan hospital, where heart specialists practiced. To make it to the U of M hospital, I had to drive an hour and twenty minutes to Lansing, drop Jonathan off at Mom's, and then drive another hour and a half to Ann Arbor.

Tired, I arrived in Ann Arbor a little after five o'clock Saturday night. I made sure I had nothing to do. I put off all of my school work until I made it back to Kalamazoo on Sunday.

I'd started a new semester at Western in early January. I was enrolled in three classes. I wanted to take more, but I had issues with my financial aid. Since I was only a sophomore, I still wasn't getting the full amount of financial aid. I didn't fret. I made sure each class I took counted toward graduation. By the end of that semester, I would have completed all of my required area courses for graduation.

Western required eight "area" courses. With my transfer classes from LCC plus my first two semesters out of the way, I had completed five out of the eight. My plan was to finish the next three "area" courses by the end of that spring 2007 semester. I was on track. After that, all I had to do was finish my proficiency courses; from then on, I would only need to complete the classes in my major.

Topaz was staying at the Ronald McDonald House. I went straight there.

I called Topaz once I pulled up. "I'm here," I said.

"Wait there," she replied. "I'm coming out. I need to go to the hospital."

I waited in my car until I spotted Topaz getting off the elevator. She walked slowly, holding her stomach as she shuffled along. Her baby weighed over eleven pounds. After many hours, the doctors decided to give her a C-section. She seemed to be holding her stitches. Hunched over, she opened my car door and slid into the passenger seat.

I drove slowly. Topaz grimaced at every bump and pothole. She cringed and held her stomach at every turn. Her honey complexion looked pale; her long, silky hair, tangled and sweaty. I felt sorry for her. On top of everything else, she was alone, with no man to help or support her.

I drove Topaz to the emergency entrance. "I need some help out here. My friend just had a baby, and she's in a lot of pain. She can't walk," I said to the first person I spotted wearing a green hospital scrub. The man grabbed a wheelchair and followed me to my car.

After Topaz was wheeled away, I went to park. Something was wrong with Topaz because she was immediately readmitted to the hospital. I waited almost three hours before I was allowed to visit Topaz in her room. I was dozing off when the nurse told me I could see her.

I stayed in the room with her for a while. I chatted, trying to lift her spirits. Topaz hadn't seen her baby all day, and she was depressed. Baby Clark's surgery was a success, but he was living breath by breath. Once he was born, the doctors had discovered that his lungs were underdeveloped as well. Even if his heart held up, there was still a strong possibility that he would stop breathing. His lungs had already collapsed twice, and so with each passing hour, it seemed more likely that he wouldn't make it.

I stayed with Topaz, keeping an eye on her. Once in the

hospital, she seemed fine. A nurse gave her medications, and she fell asleep. Growing tired, I left and went back to her room at the McDonald House. It was sometime after ten by the time I arrived.

I spent the night in the room alone. Everything seemed sad— her suitcase left open on the dresser, her hairbrush sitting on the bathroom counter, her shoes sitting next to the bed. I couldn't explain why looking at her belongings depressed me so. There were two beds in the room. I slept in the bed that was still made up.

That night, I cried for Topaz and her baby. I was coming to realize the severity of her predicament. She was now a single mom with an ill child. The child's father was locked away for an indeterminate amount of time, and she had no money. That wasn't the way I wanted her to life to end up. Topaz had been my last friend who had no children. She'd had a promising chance at a good life, and now it was gone. I knew what life was like for a single mom. It was no way for any woman to end up. I closed my eyes and tried not to think about my own baby daddy and how Grey had never been there when I needed him.

The next morning, I grabbed the items Topaz had asked me to bring and headed back to the hospital. I stayed with Topaz in her hospital room that morning. She was in good spirits, all things considered. I helped her get her swollen feet into a pair of hospital socks.

"Your hands are freezing," she said, as I tried to angle her toes into the socks.

"I know. My hands and feet are always cold. I'm a cold-blooded person."

"Damn."

I looked up at her. "I have a warm heart."

She smiled. I helped her lift her legs onto the bed. She lay down and we talked. The conversation ended up being about white women and the privileges they have because they date white men.

"I'm the only black woman up there. All the other moms in the neonatal unit have husbands. I'm the only mom there by myself. I still wear the ring that Clark gave me, but they know something's up because he hasn't been up here yet," Topaz told me.

I nodded. "It's always like that. White women always have a man by their side. When they go through somethin', they're never alone. Black women end up by their damn selves. Look at me. My baby daddy is out in the free world, and I still never see his ass. He simply doesn't want to be bothered."

Topaz sat silently for a moment, lost in our own thoughts. Then we overheard the white woman in the next bed talking loudly about her husband to some people standing around her bed side. Her husband was coming to pick her up, and she was wondering where he was.

Topaz and I exchanged glances. "She started talking 'bout her husband cause she heard us say we ain't got one," Topaz said once we were alone.

"I know. White women always tryin' ta be funny. Bitch, don't nobody care you got a damn man. You're a white woman; you're supposed to have a man. Hell, you can even get a good black man."

Topaz and I laughed a bit.

Topaz told me about the treatment she was receiving in the hospital. "I told those nurses before they discharged me that I was sick and in a lot of pain," she said. "They didn't give a damn. Ever since I've been here, they've been rude to me. They haven't listened to me. I told the nurse today that I wanted to see my baby, and she's been bullshitting me all morning. Can you get a wheelchair and take me over there?"

"You wanna go now?"

I went and found a nurse. I told her that I wanted to wheel my friend to the neonatal unit and I needed a chair. Within twenty minutes, a nurse appeared with a chair. Topaz was still hooked to an IV unit, so it took great care to get her into the chair. I pushed her slowly.

U of M hospital was enormous. One could easily get lost if he or she wasn't careful. After riding three elevators, maneuvering through two buildings, and making our way down seven massive hallways, we arrived in the neonatal intensive care unit. It was my first time in the unit. Small bodies attached to multiple machines connected by a supersystem of wires and tubes held my attention as I made my way.

The babies were the smallest I'd ever seen. They slept in small, plastic cradles. The drugs kept them quiet. Nurses and doctors busily tended to each one.

One baby was larger than all the rest. I watched him like I watched no other baby in the unit. His eyes were closed, and miniature plastic tubes led into his throat. The large patch that covered the area where his heart beat concealed several more tubes. Tubes went into his hands, and a clip with a long tube leading to a machine was attached to his big toe. The heart monitor was the only sound in the room.

I wheeled Topaz close. She leaned over and stroked her baby's leg, one of the only places on his body that didn't have a tube. Topaz wiped a tear away as she rubbed his leg. I stayed close to the door, afraid to enter. A nurse came into the room. She grabbed a chart from the edge of the plastic cradle. She checked each machine and wrote down the results.

Topaz didn't stay long. She was sick and could barely sit up in the wheelchair. Topaz asked the nurse questions about her baby, his feeding tube, and his heart. The nurse's answers were quick. The nurse seemed almost annoyed to be interrupted while doing her job.

After a few moments, Topaz asked to go back to her room. We were fairly quiet on the trip back.

"It's fucked up you gotta go through this alone," I said to Topaz. "The nurse's wouldn't be actin' like that if his dad was here."

"I know. I'm trying not to hate Clark, but I feel like he shoulda listened to me and moved to Lansing when I told him to. I could see this happening. I had a feeling."

I didn't know what to think about Topaz's situation. Even with all her cattiness, she was my best friend. I'd never told her that, though, because I was never her best friend. It hurt me to watch her, and I wanted to leave. I left the hospital around one that afternoon. It was Sunday. Jonathan and I had school the next day.

Three days later, I called Topaz. I was somewhat upset that three days had passed and she still had not called to see if we'd made it back to Kalamazoo safely. I was shocked to hear her answer.

"I just woke up from a coma," she told me. "I passed out right after you left and woke up this morning. My lungs collapsed. I was in active labor for so long that I caught an infection in my uterus. I nearly died."

No thoughts entered my mind. Never had I thought about losing Topaz. The thought of Topaz dying was too much to think about, so I pushed it out of my mind. Topaz went on to tell me about the nurses. She wanted to address the way they were treating her, but she didn't know what to do.

"It's because I'm on Medicaid," Topaz said. "They don't give a damn about you when you don't have insurance."

I agreed. When I'd had Jonathan I was covered by my dad's GM insurance. I dealt with only top-of-the-line doctors. Even though my OBGYN, Dr. Bryant, was mean to me, he'd given me excellent care.

I think he treated me badly because he was a black doctor delivering a baby to a sixteen-year-old black girl, whose family hadn't even bothered to come to one prenatal appointment. Whenever Dr. Bryant saw me, I was alone. Dr. Bryant delivered Jonathan without a word to me. He didn't even say congratulations. He silently walked out of the delivery room. I had to ask to see my son.

"You're not giving him up for adoption?" the delivery room nurse asked me.

That was the first time anyone had mentioned adoption as an option. Perhaps the thought had crossed my mind, but it hadn't stayed there. It took only a second for me to give my answer. "No. I'm keeping my baby."

I could tell Topaz was angry with me for leaving because she talked about her near-death experience during every conversation we had. I didn't feel guilty. None of her friends from Lansing— the people she'd spent all her time with—had bothered to visit her at all. All her "real friends" had disappeared, leaving only me. That bothered me.

Topaz left the Ronald McDonald House after two weeks. The organization would have let her stay at the house as long as her baby was in the hospital, but Topaz decided that she would rather commute back and forth. The doctors taking care of her baby couldn't give her any indication of when he'd be able to leave the hospital, and she was tired of being in Ann Arbor.

In March of 2007, Topaz complained that I wasn't there for her. I felt guilty, so I went back to Ann Arbor with Topaz to see her baby. He was almost four weeks old and was still in the NICU.

I dropped Jonathan off at my mom's house and headed to the East side to where Topaz lived.

Because of her baby's heart condition, Topaz chose an apartment up the street from Sparrow Hospital. As I passed Sparrow Hospital, I thought about Jonathan's birth, about the first night he'd spent cradled in my arms.

*   *   *

I'd breast-fed Jonathan as soon as he was born, and I held him on my chest for some time before I was wheeled away to my room. The first night we slept in separate rooms because the nurses wanted to let me rest. But after the first night, Jonathan slept in the room with me. On that first full night in the hospital, I got the full picture of my situation.

Jonathan refused to sleep alone. If I laid him in the bassinet, he cried. Several times, I'd nurse him and he'd fall back asleep, but as soon as he realized he was alone, he woke up crying. The only way he would sleep was on my chest.

I paged the nurse. "Can you come get the baby?" I asked. "He won't stop crying. Whenever I lay him down, he cries."

"No," she said. "You need to get used to having a baby. It's going to be like this every night."

I hated the nurses in the hospital. The next day, I went downstairs to the cafeteria to have lunch. When I came back, the nurses were giving me strange looks.

"We thought you had abandoned your baby," a nurse said to me.

"I was just downstairs having a salad," I replied.

"We paged you twice. We were about to give him some formula. He's been crying. Hurry up and get back to your room. You need to nurse your baby."

The nurse was right about one thing. I had to get used to Jonathan crying all night. I tried laying Jonathan in his crib his first night home from the hospital, and he did the same thing he'd done in the hospital. The only way I could get him to sleep was on my chest. Sometimes I worried about him rolling off me while I slept, but he never did. He fit perfectly.

Later on in life I realized that they did that to me on purpose. Perhaps they wanted me to drop him in the hospital. Or just quit and give my baby up. But I never did and never will.

* * *

Topaz and I sat in the living room smoking a blunt before we headed out to visit baby Clark. I told her I would drive so she could relax. I liked driving high on marijuana. We passed the blunt back and forth and chatted a while before we left. It was nine o'clock in the morning. We wanted to arrive in Ann Arbor early enough to spend the day there.

This visit to the U of M hospital was different. I got a chance to check out the hospital a little more. U of M was enormous, historic, and beautiful. I admired the brick streets. They reminded me of the ones in Kalamazoo and downtown Lansing.

In the NICU, I stood against the wall once again, afraid to go close to the bed. Baby Clark lay on his back, tied to the intertwined tubes connected to life-saving machines. The periodic beeping of several machines, the up-and-down motion of the ventilator, the scratch of the needle against the heart monitor—it all frightened me.

I stared at the large swathe of gauze covering the baby's chest. Underneath the gauze was his exposed heart. The doctors had to wait until he was stronger to close the wound.

I stared at Topaz's baby, and for the first time ever, I understood life—what it wanted, what it needed. Every living creature wanted to live. Every lung wanted to take a breath. Every heart wanted to beat.

Life needed caring, compassion, sacrifice, help, and love. That's exactly what baby Clark needed, and that's what he got. Man and machine fought round the clock to keep him alive. Breath after breath, he struggled to hang on.

Baby Clark was awake. He couldn't cry. No sounds could escape his throat because of the tube going to his lungs. But he wanted to cry. His scrunched his face and grimaced with every movement. Topaz and I watched in silence. Then she said, "You can move closer to the bed. He isn't gonna bite."

"I don't want to hurt him," I said.

Cautiously, I took a few steps closer. I gently stroked Clark's leg, the only place still not covered in bandages and tubes. I looked down at him. He was beautiful. He had the same toffee complexion as Topaz, the same straight, black hair and round face. He hadn't gained a pound since he was born, but he was still the biggest baby in the unit.

Baby Clark stared at Topaz, focused on her as she circled around his bed, checking his tubes. Topaz had worked as a medical assistant at a nursing home for years. She stayed on the nurse's case, overseeing her son's care. She made sure his breathing tube was inserted correctly, monitored his feeding tube, and checked his diaper.

The nurses were rude to Topaz. It was clear that they didn't respect someone who was alone, someone who was on Medicaid. I looked at the baby. He could move his head and was attentive to his surroundings. I smiled at him.

I thought to myself, *He was born eleven pounds. God made him big because he knew he was gonna fight. This baby is a fighter. He'll make it. This is his life. He wants it. He doesn't wanna die.*

Topaz and I took breaks from sitting at baby Clark's bedside. We walked around the hospital for exercise. We talked about everything and tried to find reasons to laugh. On our last break, we went to the cafeteria and ate. As we made our way back to the unit, Topaz's face turned serious.

"If he's gonna die," Topaz said to me, "I just wish he'd hurry up and do it."

I stopped walking. "He's not gonna die. He's gonna make it. He was born a big baby. Other than his heart and his lungs, he's healthy and strong. Don't worry. And don't give up. It's hard, but he'll pull through. You have to stay positive. Just keep praying."

"I wish we woulda brought the rest of that blunt."

"Me too."

Topaz and I stayed at the hospital until visiting hours were over, then we headed back to Lansing. I stopped by her house to smoke the rest of the blunt before picking up Jonathan and continuing on to Kalamazoo.

What angered me about Topaz was, even after I went to Ann Arbor twice, she still complained that I wasn't doing enough. In fact, I got the impression that she wanted me to drive to Ann Arbor and sit with her baby on the weekends, so she could get a break from doing it all week. To me, that was a job for a best friend, so I never let that conversation come to fruition. I played her from a distance.

Kristina had cut Topaz off shortly after Topaz moved to Pennsylvania in '05. I didn't have much to say about that situation. I didn't know much about Topaz and Kristina's friendship. One day, Kristina joined a Baptist church and no longer wanted to be Topaz's friend. Kristina wanted a new life, and that was that.

Topaz was a single mom, and that meant no one would sit with her baby but her. Besides, I was tired of being the only person she depended on in her time of need when she'd barely noticed I was around otherwise.

I decided to cut Topaz off a few weeks after my last visit to Ann Arbor, when I went to see baby Clark. I stopped calling and stopped answering her phone calls. In my mind, she deserved this treatment for not being there for me when I needed a friend. I had been a single mom since I was sixteen. No one had catered to me. No one had gone out his or her way for me. Life for a single mom is hard, and there is no way around it.

After a few weeks, Topaz sent me a text. She told me that we had been friends for too long for all the distance and funniness. She was right, so I called her and told her how I felt.

"You used me as a backup friend," I said. "My last year in Lansing I was completely alone. You were with Kristina and didn't bother with me. Now when times are hard for you, I'm suddenly your best friend. And where is everyone from Lansing? That night after I hung out with you and James, you changed. You started throwing card parties and didn't even invite me. I felt like it was because you were mad about him hitting on me. And you took it out on me and not him."

"I don't know what you're talking about. That night you hung out with James and me, you left after a few minutes because you said you were tired. I didn't invite you over because you didn't have a baby sitter."

Her excuse was lame. But I had something else on my mind. "And when I first bought my Cadillac, you told me that Tina

Copter and her friends would key my car up if I got my windows tinted and put rims on my car. That always bothered me because, if those are your friends, why would they fuck up my car?"

"I don't know what you're talking about. I never said that Tina would fuck your car up. If she said that to me, I would check her. But that's in the past. I wanted us to work on our friendship. I need a friend right now."

"I know you do. And when I needed a friend, I didn't have one. Now you want me to be there for you. I feel used."

Topaz and I talked again a few days later. "You're right, Nova," she said. "I was using you as a backup friend. We were never friends. We were just cool. And as far as Tina, you're just using that as an excuse."

Hearing those words put my friendship with Topaz in perspective. I still needed a true friend. I still needed someone to be down for me, and I had no one. I spent the last year of my life in Lansing alone and friendless. I no longer felt guilty about not being there for Topaz. We were "just cool"; she had told me so. I had my own life in Kalamazoo. That was that.

Sometimes I was sad about my "friend situation." I knew people in Kalamazoo, but I couldn't call them friends. I'd just met them. I'd had a boyfriend, but that didn't last.

Listening to Topaz we broke up in late March of 2007. It was shortly after I'd returned from Ann Arbor with my visit to baby Clark.

* * *

"Honestly, Nova. All your problems are because you are with that young boy. You need to break up with him, and you would feel better," Topaz told me.

We were a short-lived relationship. Aaron and I had become official shortly after I returned to Kalamazoo from Christmas break in December 2006. We were together a total of three months—my longest, consistent relationship to date.

I should have never listened to a depressed, single mom,

but I did. I listened to Tapaz's advice and ended my happiest relationship. It happened before I told Topaz about how I felt about our friendship and I'd wished that I would have let her know where we stood before I broke things off with Aaron.

Topaz was jealous of my new life and at the time I didn't see it. Once I let her know how I felt about where we stood I had a chance to reflect on her feelings about Aaron. She wished she had an Aaron in her life; A young attractive smart athlete that cared for her.

But there were other issues. Aaron was nineteen, and I was almost twenty-six. Sometimes, I felt ashamed of the age difference. Topaz played on that.

After I broke up with Aaron, I realized that, despite the age difference, we were right for each other. I called Aaron the next day and apologized.

He accepted my apology. Then two days later, we broke up again.

"I'm takin' us off Facebook," Aaron told me over the phone.

"Why?" I asked, pissed.

"Cause, I was talkin' to my best friend about us. She was like, 'You should take her off Facebook.'"

"You have a best friend who's a girl? If she's such a good friend, why haven't I heard of her?"

Aaron began mumbling under his breath.

"So you're breaking up with me?" I asked.

"You broke up with me, remember?"

"That was two days ago. I called you and said sorry. You said you were over it."

"Why you trippin' cause I wanna take us off Facebook?"

"Cause, you're on a public site saying that you have a girlfriend. Now you want to announce that you're single." I wasn't going to argue with Aaron. If he wanted to take us off Facebook, then I would let him. "Go on and take it off. I don't give a fuck. You wanna listen to some bitch about me, then listen to her."

We argued back and forth, but it was over. My first college

relationship had ended. I would no longer be spending my nights in Draper Hall. It was the first time in my life that I saw clearly how other people had destroyed a relationship that was mine.

I promised myself that, if I ever built up another relationship, I wouldn't let other people tear it down.

*   *   *

During this time Green seemed to be the only thing working out for me. He had been renting my condo for nearly three months, and I'd had no problems with the situation. He paid his rent on time. I was grateful for that because, even though I'd been released from work back in November, Workers Comp hadn't started paying me again until mid-February. Green's rent money was how I survived. I used that money just to eat.

CHAPTER ELEVEN:
An Unexpected Phone Call

ON TUESDAY, MARCH 17, 2007, I received an unexpected phone call from my mom. "Nova, the police were here today," she said. "They were looking for you."

I knew right then something terrible was going to happen to me. The police never went looking for a person unless it was something serious. Most times, people went looking for the police.

I called the officer who'd left his business card with my mom. I gave him my address in Kalamazoo, and he sent me a letter.

The letter was a notice of eviction directed at Green and his two roommates. I called the number on the bottom of the notice and talked to a man named Brian, who said he was the attorney for my condo association.

I couldn't believe the things Brian told me. He informed me of numerous noise violations, disruptive company, pets not under control. I called Maple Grove Property Management, who was managing Fairfield at the time, as soon as I got off the phone.

I spoke with Danny Walsh, who was handling my case at the time. Danny sounded as if he was expecting to hear from me. He let out a loud sigh, and I heard the faint rustling of papers.

"There's been a whole lot a trouble at the condo," he said, as he pulled up my file.

And he was right. There was a lot whole lot of trouble going on at my condo—so much so that over three thousand dollars in fines had been charged to me by the condominium association. According to Danny, the condo association had been sending notices of violations of a number of bylaws. However, I'd never seen any of these notices.

According to Maple Grove, Green was destroying the condo community with his dogs, company, loud music, and excessive vehicles. This was shocking news to me. I never imagined that Green would destroy my house, but you can never know a person until you let him or her move in.

I had Danny send me copies of all the violation records.

After I received the seven-inch packet in the mail, I picked up the phone and punched in my brother's phone number.

"Green," I said, "I'm getting a bunch of violation notices because of you. What's going on?"

"Nothing. I haven't got anything," he said.

"They haven't given you any copies of the violations?"

"No."

What the fuck is going on? How is Green racking up thousands of dollars worth of violations and fines without me being notifyied.

"Well it's almost three thousand dollars right now. I'm not gonna pay for this. These are your violations, and you are responsible. If you don't understand, read the lease we signed."

"Don't worry, I'll pay for 'em. I'ma talk to Book and News tonight when they get home."

I let my anger subside. I had too much stress at school to deal with this new problem. Besides, I didn't know how to handle things.

All three tenants agreed to split the costs of the violations. I didn't worry, as long as I didn't have to pay. The boys seemed sympathetic to my plight and acted as if they would rectify the situation as quickly as possible.

Then Green skipped April's rent, and then May's. Both Book and News withheld their portions of the violations until Green paid his portion of the rent. Usually they gave the money to Green and then green made the deposit into my account. However now they refused to pay. All the while, the mortgage on the condo still had to be paid.

I paid the mortgage, though I was just barely able to. All my savings were depleted by the end of May.

Losing money is the worst feeling in the world. One can lose a spouse or a loved one and still feel as if he or she can make it through the day. But to lose money makes a person feel helpless. When the funds dwindle to nearly nothing, you feel as if in the next blink of an eye, you might find yourself at someone else's mercy, unable to afford to take care of yourself.

I had to do something about the situation with Green. He wasn't paying his portion of the rent, and the violations were mounting. I went to Lansing June 1, 2007. I brought with me all of the violations and a copy of the first eviction notice, as well as the second, which by this time, named me as well.

"Have you received any of these violations?" I asked Green while surveying my condo.

In the living room and dining room everything looked normal as far as I could see. There were no dogs, no heavy traffic; not even the roommates were there.

I sat in the living room and surveyed the scene. I didn't do a walk-through right then because I wanted Green to have space and privacy. I didn't want to be the overbearing sister who used the fact that she was the landlord to rule over her little brother. I never had a landlord come over to my apartment and walk around, so I gave Green the same respect. That was one of my biggest mistakes.

If I would have looked around, I would have gotten a better understanding of the situation. Instead, I took my brother's word that he had everything under control and left it alone.

Being back in the condo brought back memories. The furniture was different, but everything else remained the same. I thought about Grey and the days we'd spent in the condo, talking and hanging out.

I shook my head and pushed those thoughts and feelings aside. I was in a new place doing what I always wanted to do. College was a new chapter, and I had to focus on that.

I placed the seven-inch packet of violations on the coffee table in front of Green. I grabbed a violation from the top of the pile and began reading: "Excessive noise, one hundred dollars." I grabbed another violation and read: "Too many vehicles at the residence, one hundred dollars, fifth notice." I picked up another violation: "Not cleaning up after pets, one hundred dollars, eighth notice."

Green looked at me, sincerity in his eyes. "Nova, I don't have a car. We have two parking spots. Book and News use those. As far as the noise, no one is ever here. We clean up after our dogs. Right now, there's not even a dog here."

"Have you received any of these violations?"

"No, nobody told me anything," he said, sitting across from me, focused and determined to help me sort out the mishap.

I believed him. Green would never do what the violations said he'd done. He was my closet sibling. Not only were we brother and sister, we were friends. I trusted him.

"I got another notice in the mail yesterday. Now they're trying to evict me from my condo too. I have to be out by June 15."

"What! Can they do that?" he asked, sounding shocked.

"I don't know. You know what I think? I think it's because we're black, and they don't want us out here," I continued. "When I lived out here, I thought they were funny actin'. They splashed me every summer when I was at the pool. Remember last summer when that white guy splashed us then started laughing?"

I'd begun having problems with a few of my neighbors who lived across the street from me. For the most part I ignored them until I began having problems with being splashed at the pool. The man that splashed me lived in one of the houses across the street and he and his family watched me often.

My mind flashed to an image of a tall, white man with a lean body and a slight belly bulge diving headfirst into the pool and sending a large wave up and over the side of the pool and onto Green and me. I sat drenched. My hair and face wet, and I was pissed.

The man's family laughed. Then they began talking. I couldn't understand what they said because they were Czechoslovakian, and they only spoke Slovak in front of me. I knew they were Czechoslovakian because one of the boys from their family was a playmate of my son, and he told Jonathan that he was Czechoslovakian.

Pissed, I got up from the side of the pool and went over to them. With a cold smile, I introduced myself to them. "Hi, my name is Nova," I said.

I remained smiling, even though I wanted to spit on them.

They told me their names. I only partially understood them because of their heavy accents. They smiled and said hello, even though I could tell they felt awkward. They didn't expect me to get up and come over.

The best way to face evil is head on. I could have ignored them like most people, but why? Why should I not enjoy myself on a hot summer day when I spend my money to be out there just like them? I owned the pool the same as they did, and that was a hard fact that they were going to have to face.

What upset me the most was the fact that the same man had splashed Topaz and me the summer before. Immediately after the water hit me, I let him know how I felt. "Don't ever splash me again," I told him. The next summer, the same thing happened. I guess he didn't get the message.

Green looked at me; he cocked his head to the side and then lowered it. "Yeah, I mean, I haven't had any problems out here personally," he said, "but I can't think of anything that it could be. I'm telling you, we haven't been doing shit out here. I go to work and come home. Book and News, they don't do shit at the house."

Green wasn't as convinced as me. That's because he was only nineteen. If he was older, he would have understood white people and the games they played.

"I don't think they can evict me from my condo, and I don't think they can evict you either. I have an appointment with an attorney this afternoon, so we'll see what she says."

"Cool," Green said.

"Okay, now that we got that taken care of, let's talk about my money. Where is it? I told you I can't afford for you to keep paying your rent late. You're behind three months. I'm behind on my rent back in Kalamazoo. I can't afford to pay your way."

"I know. I know. I'm trying to get it together. I just got a new job, and I've been working. I should have five hundred for you in two weeks."

"Two weeks. Green, if you're not caught up by June 15, I want you to leave."

Green stared at me as if my threat was an astonishing blow. I gave him a stern look, never taking my eyes off him.

"Okay," he said, otherwise silent.

"Okay." I stood to leave. "I'll get at you later." I paused; I couldn't think of anything else to say.

Green closed the door quietly behind me.

I left my meeting with Green with a feeling that he wasn't going to be able to pay me. Immediately I placed a phone call to Book.

"Hey Book," I said.

"Sup?" he asked.

"Nothing, I just wanted to talk to you about something. As you know, Green has been behind on his rent. I told him that if he didn't pay by the fifteenth, I wanted him to move out. You and your brother have been good renters to me, so, I'm offering you two the opportunity to sign a new lease, without Green."

A short pause ensued. "Uh, well, I have to talk to my brother first, but we might be willing to do it."

"Okay. Now you know that you guys will still be responsible for the full amount of the rent—seven fifty—right?"

"Okay, yeah, let me talk to him and see what he says."

"All right, let me know by the first of July."

Despite my rights as a homeowner, panic began to set in. I didn't know all the clauses in the condo association bylaws; in fact, I had never read the bylaws. I was not aware of the rights of the condo association. I had so many questions. If the association decided to evict me and my tenants, would I still be responsible for the mortgage? What would GMAC, my mortgage company, have to say? What would I do if my condo had to sit empty? I couldn't afford the mortgage without any rental income.

My mind raced from one scenario to another; each outcome looked grim and dismal. Even if Green left and Book and News stayed, the brothers had no documented income. On the other hand, if all three of them left, I'd have no rental income until I found a new renter.

I thought about my options, as well as my limitations, as I made my way to my first visit with Jenny, my new attorney.

I drove up and down Grand Street looking for building 200. Jenny was located in Old Town. Old Town was just streets away from downtown Lansing. Old Town was very old; the area was home to some of the oldest buildings in Lansing. The streets were still paved with brick. The buildings were small but well cared for. All in all, Old Town was beautiful.

I walked into building 200 and fell in love with the décor. The office was done in the same yellow as my condo, giving it a trendy feel. Some of the walls were brick; other sections had been cleverly painted to have an antique look and feel. I gave the receptionist my name and took a seat in the waiting lobby.

"Hi, I'm Jenny," said an overweight, white woman with blond, shoulder-length hair.

We shook hands, and I introduced myself. I looked Jenny over. She was young for an attorney and I could tell that she was just starting out. Even though she was a novice, I liked her.

Jenny sat across from me. She was friendly but serious. She listened closely.

"They can't evict you from your condo," she told me after listening to my story. "That's illegal. They're trying to scare you."

She read over the violations.

"Can they evict my brother?" I asked.

"No, but they can continue to cite you so that you will evict him."

Then I understood. I was right. They didn't want to live across the street from a house full of black men, so they were coming after me. Someone had to stop them.

"Can I handle this on my own?"

She looked at me with regret in her eyes. "Unfortunately, no. They've already started the eviction process. Even though they can't legally evict you they've begun the paperwork. They can take this all the way to court and charge you a lot of money in the process…What I will do if you decide to go with me is contact Brian and let him know that you have an attorney working on your case."

"How much would you charge to take on a case like this?"

"I would need a thousand-dollar retainer to get started."

Fuck, a thousand dollars. But if I don't do it, they might actually find a way to evict me from my house, and then what?

"I don't have a thousand dollars. I can pay you two fifty now and two fifty every other week."

Jenny looked at me. "I usually don't do this. I'm still paying off my student loans." She gave me a hard stare. "I don't want to have to come after you for my money."

"You won't. I'll pay you."

I had told Jenny that I was a student as well. I had student loans from Western. I understood the dilemma of paying back student loans. Between financial aid and my GM tuition reinvestment, I'd virtually had my associate's degree paid for. My bachelor's degree was a different story. I had only been at Western three semesters and already owed over $12,000.

Jenny's receptionist wrote up a contract stating our payment arrangement. I signed it and wrote Jenny a check for $250.

A few days later, I got a call from Jenny. Fairfield was stopping the eviction. They were upset that Green would be staying, but they had no control over who I rented my condo to. I told Jenny that I would pay them. I thought the matter was resolved.

July 1 passed with no payment from Green. On July 2, I sent him a formal eviction notice. I was proud of the eviction notice. It was professional. I got it from the landlord kit I'd purchased from Staples in late June, when I realized that I had no idea how to properly manage my condo. A book was always a great place to start. I flipped through the landlord kit. In black and white were the rules to landlording.

I should have done my research before I decided to take over from the management company. I should have known what I was getting into. I read the entire manual from cover to cover and learned how to deal with Green and my future tenants.

One of the first rules to being a landlord was to research the tenant thoroughly before letting him or her move in.

Originally, I wanted Green to be out by August 1. However, after I talked to Book again, I decided to have Green move at the end of August.

Both Book and News opted not to renew their lease with me. Since neither one of them had signed the current lease, I made Green stay in the condo until they moved out. I figured that I needed someone there whose name was on the lease. Never again would I let someone move into my condo without being on the lease.

During June and July, I received more violations from Fairfield Place. Now that the association had my address in Kalamazoo, I received at least one packet of violations in the mail every other weekend. The violations never came as an individual notice; rather, they came in a bundle of at least three. The association would figure out three or four different ways to cite me for each alleged occurrence.

My anxiety grew; soon I would have a panic attack whenever I heard an unexpected knock on my door, sure that it was the mailman with a certified letter from Fairfield. All my friends called before they came over.

I called Green every time I received a violation. Every time, he offered the same line—nothing was wrong. I became convinced that the association was inventing these violations because of the color of our skin.

If I had a loving, caring family, I could have called my dad, grandma, sister, or Earnest and asked one of them to go check on Green. But since Mom's stroke, Yellow and I barely talked, and Dad didn't want to be bothered. Grandma was too busy helping the needy in the family, so I didn't call her. Earnest came to visit me once in Kalamazoo about a month after I had moved there and all he did was complain about issues he was having with Yellow. I then told him that Kalamazoo was a peaceful place and not to bring his problems with him. He was pissed and after that we no longer kept in contact. I had to take Green's word.

If Green would have paid his rent, I would have allowed him to stay just to prove to the association that they had no power over me. However, since Green refused to pay, I moved forward with the eviction. I placed an advertisement for a new renter on Michiganlocator.com, a Web site I found out about when I called HUD looking for Section 8 renters.

I put my condo on the market on August 1. I found a new renter in two days. Her name was Keydah Cowern. She was a twenty-eight-year-old black female with three children and no husband. I spoke to Keydah on the phone. We agreed to meet at the condo for a showing on August 8.

Dealing with Green and the condo consumed my life. The only relief I got was that my grades were good, and I was released from academic probation after the summer 1 2007 semester.

When I had received a letter in May saying that I would be expelled from school if I didn't raise my grades, I'd panicked I had forgotten that grades were my number one priority.

My promise to myself to maintain a high GPA this time around had been pushed to the back of my mind. I skipped class whenever I felt like it. I was tired half the time and stressed out the other half.

My poor attendance drastically hurt my grades. In addition,

I didn't like the area of study I'd chosen as my major. I no longer wanted to me a human resource manager, so after the spring semester ended, I switched my major to English/creative writing. I decided that I wanted to pursue writing as a career.

I made sure to never skip class unless there was a true emergency. I promised myself that, no matter what, I would make it to class.

I loved being in the English department. I felt as if I was making progress toward my writing career. Even though I had never found a publisher for my first book, I'd begun writing a second novel in September 2006. The book was about a young girl with a troubled past who got a new start when she went off to college.

I didn't finish the book. My computer crashed when I was on page one hundred. Unfortunately, I hadn't backed up the book, and so I lost it. I was crushed but inspired.

I finally understood Eric Jerome Dickey's advice. It was time to learn my craft. I gave English my all. I tried to remember everything I learned in public school, and I was eager to learn more.

English was a hard major. It required lots of reading and writing, and all the literature we studied was hard, college-level work. The papers were long and hard, but English was my gift, along with history. In high school, I'd always aced both the English and social studies sections of the SAT and other standardized tests.

My high school diploma had an English endorsement from the governor of Michigan because my tests scores were so high. It was only natural that I ended my first semester with the English department on the Dean's List. I made the Dean's List during Summer II semester as well.

I dropped my business minor. I chose Africana studies as a second major. I loved the African American history class I took in the spring 2007 semester. It would be difficult to double major, but I could do it. Remembering dates and names came easy to me.

On August 8, Keydah and I walked in my condo as we had planned. The first thing I noticed was the smell of dog shit and the new pit bull sitting on the back deck. I took a swallow and continued smiling as I showed Keydah around.

Green was there cleaning up, or at least trying to. I gave him more than enough notice; he should have had the place ready. Pissed, I walked by him. He said "Hi," to Keydah and me. I barely spoke back.

Every room was nasty. The tan carpet in the living room had turned black; the Venetian-blinds were twisted and broken. The kitchen was hidden in dirty dishes, old food, and spilled drinks that no one had bothered to clean up. My feet stuck to the tile floor. I opened the refrigerator. Steak blood seeped from the top shelf to the bottom drawers; the freezer was the same.

The handle had been ripped off the microwave. My ceramic stovetop was coved in baked-on grime. I ran my fingers over the surface, convinced that it would never come clean.

In the finished basement, dog shit stained my carpet. I poked my head through a large hole in the door separating the laundry room from the main room. The grate was busted off. There were too many piles of clothes to show Keydah the laundry room.

"Don't worry about all of this. I'm gonna make sure that everything is fixed and cleaned up before you move in," I told her.

"Oh, I'm not thinking 'bout all that. I love this place. It's beautiful," she said, as we watched our step while we climbed the littered stairs.

The upstairs bedrooms had clothes strewn from one end to the other. The upstairs bathroom had a large, black ring around the tub. Soot and grit covered the floor, sink, and toilet.

Despite the condition of the condo, Keydah still wanted to rent from me. "Give me a week to run your credit and check everything out," I told her.

She looked somewhat disappointed but said, "Okay, just let me know."

I knew right then that she would be my next renter, but I wanted her to wait. I didn't want to be too desperate. Plus, I needed to run her credit and criminal background. She'd told me about her past credit problems. She'd gotten behind on credit cards. But she assured me that she had no evictions and had a strong work history. She didn't lie. Everything checked out.

I ran her credit with the information on her application. Just like she said, the only negative marks were unpaid credit cards. She had no criminal record, and her job checked out. I called her on August 15 to give her the news. She was ecstatic to hear that she would be the next person in my condo.

We decided on October 1 as her move-in date. She would meet me at the condo on August 23 to give me the $500 I charged her as a deposit. The money also ensured her that I would hold the condo for her.

Green would be leaving on August 31. That would give me one month to turn the place around. I called Green that night to let him know that I had found a new renter. We went over the plans and decided I would collect my keys and do a final walk-through on the thirty-first.

As if the continuous violations weren't enough, I received an updated fine list from the association the day before I went to Lansing to collect my deposit from Keydah. In a week, Green was to be out for good.

I screamed when I read the final balance—$10,815.23. I called my attorney, frantic and pacing. Jenny assured me that she would talk to Brian again. She told me that the charges were excessive and that she could talk them down. All I could do was wait.

Keydah brought her daughter with her to see the condo when she brought me my deposit. The condo was in worse shape than it had been before. More dirt and trash had piled up; more repairs awaited me. I couldn't stop thinking about the $10,000 fine as I showed my new renters around. I could tell from the look on the little girl's face that she didn't want to live there. All she saw was grime.

"Don't worry. All of this will be cleaned up and fixed before you move in," I told her smiling.

She didn't smile back. I didn't expect her to.

CHAPTER TWELVE:
The Turnover

ON THE DAY OF my final walk-through with Green and his roommates, Jonathan and I stopped by my mom's house. Jonathan went upstairs to see my mom and I went into the basement to where Green and my brother Earnest were.

"Can you take me to the condo with you?" Green asked.

"Sure, I'll be leaving here in about thirty minutes," I said, finishing my conversation with Earnest.

Earnest and I sat in his studio he had built in my mom's basement talking. Earnest sat at his keyboard facing the sound room with the large microphone. I glanced into the sound room, no one was there. Usually a rapper stood behind the large glass window facing out toward earnest and his keyboard. Today the booth sat empty.

I'd found one of Green's blunts on the kitchen counter and was smoking it. I told Green I would pay him five dollars for the blunt and I did. It just so happened that I had found a five dollar bill lying around and I paid him with that.

Green watched silently. I had already told him he couldn't smoke with me. I was never smoking with him again. Since Earnest didn't smoke marijuana I had the blunt all to myself.

Green sat watching me for a few minutes and then went up stairs. He had made a phone call to a friend of his and was in the process of purchasing a dime bag of weed for himself. He was gone a few minutes and then came back into the basement.

He reached into his pocket and fingered the five dollar bill I'd just given him. "Hey, has anyone seen my five dollar bill I left on the diningroom table?" he asked.

"I did. I gave it to you to pay for this blunt," I told him.

"That was my five dollars. I needed that to pay for my dime bag."

"Well, I'm not giving you another five dollars." I gave him a blank stare and continued smoking.

"So you paid me with my own money?"

"Yeah. You're gonna pay for those violations you left me with." I thought for a moment then smiled. "I'ma get my money in tens and twenties," I said exhaling a large billow of smoke.

Earnest and I exploded in laughter. Green gave me a half smile and nodded his head. I knew then that some way he would pay for what he had done to me and there would be nothing he could do about it.

"That's fucked up that they would try to charge you so much," Earnest said taking a break from his keyboard.

Earnest turned to me. He rubbed his thin mustache as he thought the situation over.

"I know. I can't believe that the bill is over ten thousand dollars. I mean, I have to pay the association damn near seven thousand in attorney fees." I shook my head in disbelief.

"Damn," Earnest said. He turned back to his keyboard. He fiddled with a new beat he was working on. I listened to the instrumental, impressed with his talent.

I shot a sideways glance at Green on the other side of the room. "I hope that there's something my attorney can do to get me outta this."

Perhaps the situation was too much for Green to bear. He dismissed himself, "I'ma go wait for you outside," he said.

"Fine." I turned back to Earnest.

Earnest stared at me with a hard look in his eyes. Out of nowhere he said, "Yeah, you were fuckin' with Green, and now look what happened."

Earnest continued his menacing stare. "I wanted to rent the condo from you, and you didn't give me a chance. Now look."

A flash of anger caused my forehead to sweat. I patted my face and began scratching the back of my neck. "What are you talking about?" I asked. "You said you wanted to move in March, I couldn't afford to wait three months for you. Besides, why are you bringing this up now? It's over now. If you wanted to say something, you shoulda said something a long time ago."

"I'm not even trying to say something. I'm just mentioning the fact that you're sitting here, holding a ten-thousand-dollar bill, and it's because you were so busy trying to help Green when you knew that I wanted the condo…"

"What?" I said exalted.

I knew where Earnest was going. He was jealous because I'd given the condo to Green and not him. And then when everything went to hell, he decided to use my moment of weakness to let me know how big a fool I'd been for not waiting on him.

"Well," I continued. "I don't know why you're waiting until now to bring the shit up, I said, realizing that I'd made a mistake letting my family become a part of my personal life.

I stood to leave. I looked at Earnest, tall and handsome, with smooth, brown skin; short waves in his low-cut Caesar; and a six-pack, he was intelligent and such a waste of a black man.

"I'm leaving now," I said. "Just remember, when you didn't have shit, I was there for you. When your baby was born, I went out and bought a nice ass stroller, a car seat, and clothes and gave you money. You didn't get the condo because you waited too long. You were scared to step out and take that step on your own, and Green beat you to it."

I walked upstairs to get my son before leaving. Earnest's words had hurt, but I shook the disappointment off.

Green was waiting for me on the front steps. I avoided making eye contact with him. We climbed inside my CTS, and I accelerated out of the driveway.

I thought that perhaps he had tried to clean up the condo because, during the car drive, he requested the return of his $200 deposit.

"You left me with over ten thousand dollars worth of damage," I replied. "You're not getting shit back." I gave him an evil look.

I went inside my condo followed by Jonathan and then Green. Book and News were there, along with several other people I didn't recognize. No one had started to move out. I felt the walls closing in on me. I started at each of the men, pissed, trying to control my anger. I checked my watch; it was 11:15.

Green, feeling as if he needed to say something, broke the silence. "Look, I just wanted to say that I'ma take care of everything. I'll pay for the violations. Book and News"—he turned to face his friends—"I mean, the two of you have carried me for a while. I'ma be a man and pay for it."

You damn right you gonna pay for it. You stupid boy, I'm gonna sue your punk ass. You gonna pay for all this shit cause ain't nobody else to pay for it.

I stared at Green. There was no point in me staying right then. "I'll be back at one. Someone from Lowe's is coming to look at the basement door," I said. I turned to the two brothers. I wasn't mad at them I had no reason to be. I hadn't put them on the lease. They were free to go. "I have my people coming in here tomorrow morning. If you're stuff isn't out, I'ma sit it on the curb."

"Can I come with you? I need to go back to the West," Green asked.

"Fine."

We piled back into my car. I tried to forget about my condo, yet it was all I could think about. "Green, where's my rent money?"

"I don't have it right now. I'll have it to you by five o' clock."

"What! What the fuck do you mean you don't have it?" I yelled. The rent money was the only reason I'd remained calm.

* * *

I started calling Book every day once August 15 had passed because neither Book nor his brother had paid August's rent. They didn't answer their phone nor return my calls. Pissed I kept up my harassment by calling them everyday. Since I knew Book a little better than news I called him more often. The last message I left on Book's answering machin finally got me a response.

I called Book's phone and said, "This is Nova. I'm calling because I still haven't received you or your brother's portion of the rent. I know you aren't gonna do that to me. I know you aren't gonna stiff me and not pay August's rent." I paused then added, "Give me a call back."

That was the most direct message I had left thus far. Before that I was being nice and stayed brief on the phone.

Book called me back to let me know that he had $500 of the rent for him and his brother; Green's portion was missing. I told him to drop what he had off at my mom's that night. That was Sunday. Usually, rent was deposited into my account, but because of the way things were ending, I no longer wanted to take chances.

By Tuesday, my mom had not received the rent money. I called Henery again; he claimed Green called him and picked it up right before he went to take it to my mom. Green always handled the rent, so he trusted Green with the money. Immediately, I called Green. He claimed that he would deposit the money into my account that day. By Thursday, he still had not made the deposit. I called him again and told him to hold onto the money, and I would pick it up when I came to get my keys that Friday.

*   *   *

Unable to believe he was once again telling me he didn't have the money, I asked again, "Where the fuck is my money?"

"I told you, I will have it by five o'clock."

"No the fuck you won't. Where the fuck is your broke ass gonna get five hundred dollars by five o'clock? Be honest. You stole my five hundred dollars, didn't you?"

Technically he owed me seven hundred and fifty dollars but since I knew he wasn't going to have his portion of the rent I only pressed him for the five hundred Book and News had paid.

"I didn't steal your five hundred dollars."

"Then where the fuck is it? You muthafuckin', bitch-ass nigga, you stole my five hundred dollars on the last fuckin' day, after you ran up ten thousand dollars worth of violations and after you trashed my condo. You punk ass, crackhead, bitch."

Crying, I called my sister, Asia, "Asia, you won't guess what the fuck has happened to me. Green's punk ass has stole my five hundred dollars. After his bitch ass just trashed my fuckin' house. I knew his punk ass wasn't shit."

"Can you let me out the car?" Green asked, rolling his eyes.

"No, you're gonna sit here and listen, you thieving son of a bitch," I screamed.

Green wanted to get out of the car so he could get away from me. If I let him go, he would simply avoid me until things blew over. Green was going to get the cursing out of his life, and I wasn't going to say anything directly to him. He sat quietly as I continued. "I can't believe this shit has happened to me. I want to stab his fuckin' ass."

Asia consoled me. "No, Nova, you can't do that," she said. "I told you that Green wasn't shit. He came down here to Nashville and ran up my phone bill over a thousand dollars calling psychic numbers. Then he stole from me—took three hundred out my purse. Green ain't shit. No one ever listens to me. I told you all that."

"I don't remember what he did to you. All I remember is that he came back to Lansing with a cut-up neck."

"Yeah he came back with a cut-up neck. He cussed me out, told me I wasn't shit, after all I did for him. So I jumped on him and cut up his neck with my clippers. Green ain't shit."

"I know. He don't wanna do shit but smoke weed and lay around all day. Punk ass bitch."

Through the tears, I watched the road. Driving faster, I continued my rant. Green remained silent as Asia and I continued our conversation. As each city block passed, my anger grew. I screamed and cursed, and yet nothing made me feel better. I began imagining myself pushing Green out the car. I wanted to kill him. I began screaming at the top of my lungs and banging on the steering wheel.

"Mom!" Jonathan yelled from the back seat.

Remembering my son and all that I had left, I pulled over to the side of the road. I turned and faced Green. "Get the fuck out my car," I said, refraining from slapping him in the face.

Without a word, Green opened the passenger door and got out.

"Oh God, I feel better already. I just needed to get that evil spirit away from me," I said to Asia.

"Who were you just talking to?" she asked.

"Green, I told you he was still in the car."

"You still gave him a ride. See, that's why this happened to you. If it was me, I would have kicked his ass out. I wouldn't of gave him a ride home. You're so stupid; you're always being nice."

At that moment, my hate toward Green turned to Asia, "What the fuck are you talking about? At least I have a condo to cry over. You've been homeless for two years. Fuck you, Asia" I screamed into the phone. I closed my flip phone, ending our conversation.

With no family around, I had a moment to think. I realized that helping during my years of prosperity had destroyed me. I had been left financially, emotionally, and spiritually crippled. What tormented me the most was that I couldn't understand why. I had done nothing but good for Green. I'd let him live with me when our dad kicked him out. I'd let him drive my brand new Cadillac CTS to school. I'd given him money. I'd always treated him with kindness and respect.

Dazed, I ended up at Mom's house. I parked my car and used my spare key to let myself in. I marched up the stairs. "Mom, get up," I said, crying so hard I was barely able to talk.

"What's wrong?" she asked, sitting up.

Still crippled from her stroke, the left side of her body was unable to function. I stared at her drooped lips and sagging face—a feeble attempt at life. She was pitiful.

"Green left my house fucked up. There's shit broken and trash everywhere. He tore the handle off my microwave. His dog ripped up the carpet in the upstairs bedroom."

Mom looked stunned. "Oh no," she said.

I stared at her, pissed and frustrated. My intention was to scream and yell at her, but I didn't have the heart. She tried to stand up straight. It was the way her hand shook that made me stop. "I'm leaving, I'm going to cuss out my dad," I said, deciding to battle with someone worth fighting.

Jonathan stared at me, quiet and unsure. He looked over at mom, realizing that she had no power to stop me. No one did. At that moment I was so pissed that I wasn't afraid of anything or anyone. I left my son with my mom because I didn't want him to see what was coming. He had seen enough.

I tried to calm down as I spoke to Mom, yet the anger reigned. I couldn't stop cursing. "Green that no-good, coke snorting, thieving, crackhead. He ain't gonna do shit but end up in rehab," I said, as I stomped out of her room. And then I lost it.

"Rehab. Rehab. Rehab," I screamed, as I banged on the wall while I stormed down the stairs.

* * *

The month of September became a blur. I had to maintain my grades at Western while I fixed my condo. Deep into my English major, I had to become two people—the Lansing me and the Kalamazoo me.

I took four classes that semester. Among them was my first four thousand–level course—*Studies in the Novel*.

Studies in the Novel was especially difficult because of the vocabulary in some of the literature we studied. The first four novels were written in Old English. I struggled because I didn't understand many of the words. Sometimes I had to skip whole sections because I didn't know the meaning of the words.

I experienced the same difficulty in class. Sometimes I barely knew what the professor was saying because his vocabulary was of a higher level than mine.

I felt dumb because many of the other students knew the words the professor used. I had to listen dumbfounded as students just like me "word dropped"—that is spoke in lengthy sentences loaded up with big words. For the first time in my life, I wished I had paid more attention during English in middle and high school.

That's how it was in the English department. The vocabulary level was high, and no one dumbed it down just because I was there. No one spoke in Ebonics, and there were no dictionaries in the classroom. If I didn't know all of the words being said, I had to do my best to understand. And if I still couldn't keep up, then perhaps I needed to pick another major.

I prayed constantly and sometimes went to church. I was confused about who I was and had no clue what my purpose in life was. But I kept going. A constant feeling in the back of my mind told me that, no matter what, I had to keep going.

Every weekend, I booked a hotel room on Priceline.com. Whenever possible, I tried to avoid my family when I went to Lansing. I couldn't wait for them to change. I realized that, if I wanted peace, I had to get it myself.

I devised an efficient plan to complete the turnover of the apartment. Each week after I finished up my classes at school, I'd load my car with cleaning supplies and head to Lansing. I'd spend the entire weekend cleaning, scrubbing, patching, and painting.

Topaz, a friend of mine, gave me her cousin, Crystal's, phone number. Crystal cleaned houses, and I was complaining to Topaz on the phone that I didn't know what to do. I had no idea how I was going to put everything back together.

I called Crystal and told her my dilemma. She accepted the job. I met Crystal on Saturday September 1, the day after Green and his roommates moved out. Crystal arrived at exactly nine o'clock in the morning. I watched her from the living room window as she climbed out of an old, green van. An older, white woman was driving. Crystal waved the woman away as she made her way to the front door.

"Crystal," she said, shaking my hand.

I invited her inside. She took a look around and shook her head.

"Yeah, I know. My brother did this to me," I said, sadly.

Crystal had soft, brown eyes. Large, auburn curls fell to her shoulders. She kept the strands at bay with a large headband. Crystal looked to be in her mid-thirties.

I didn't know what would be harder to repair—the three rooms upstairs or the basement. I decided to take the upstairs. I wanted to clean the bedrooms myself.

For the first day, I didn't see Crystal much. I stayed upstairs digging through trash of all sorts and old clothes. I threw everything away. That made the job go a lot faster. Once all the rooms were cleaned out, I moved onto cleaning the bathroom. Then I began painting.

At one o'clock, I wanted a break. I also wanted to check on Crystal.

"Wow," I said when I saw the basement.

Crystal had everything cleaned up. She'd even washed the basement walls and cleaned all the spiderwebs from the ceiling. There were still a few large items in the basement that Green left, including his couch and computer desk.

"Don't worry about that," I said, pointing to the large items. "I'm gonna have a trash removal company come get those."

"I was thinking that you should paint the basement all white. That would make the room look bigger," Crystal told me.

Usually I just did the trim, but I decided that Crystal was right. "That's a great idea," I said.

I broke open the white paint and gave Crystal a few paint brushes, and she got started. I told her to take a break whenever she wanted and turned to go back upstairs to finish with the rooms.

"It must be a lot of work cleaning the upstairs. I can imagine how the bedrooms look," Crystal said.

I turned back around. I gave her a stressed look. "It is," I said.

And it was.

At the end of the day, I went back down to the basement. Wide-eyed, I looked around. Crystal had finished painting, cleaned all the brushes, and put everything away.

"I don't know what I woulda done without you. Thank you," I told her as I looked around.

Crystal left at exactly five o'clock with a promise to return at nine the next morning. I didn't leave with Crystal. I stayed and cleaned until my shoulders hurt too much to lift them.

While I cleaned I thought about Green lying around asleep on the other side of town while I scrambled to put my house back in order. The thought made me hate him even more, so I thought about other things to keep me busy.

Grey was on my mind for many hours as I finished with the upstairs. I drove past his old house on my way back to the West side to pick up Jonathan. Seeing the place nearly brought tears to my eyes. It was hard to imagine that, just a little over a year ago, he was in my life, my best friend. It seemed as if my life with Grey would never end, yet it did.

I left the condo at sundown and went to my mom's house and picked up Jonathan then we went to the hotel.

Jonathan and I went swimming at the hotel that night. We splashed in the pool at the Marriot in East Lansing and forgot about why we were there. We played Marco Polo. We competed to see who could hold his or her breath under water the longest.

"I'm glad we got a room," Jonathan said, as he floated on the rubber tube while I pulled him around the large, indoor pool.

"Me too," I said, looking out at the sundeck.

There is no drama when a person has a place of their own to stay. Being in another person's house gives away your power. If I would have stayed with a family member I would have been forced to deal with their comments and listen to their perspective on my situation. In the end there would have been nothing but arguing and fighting. I was happy I was on my own and doing things my way.

I slept peacefully that night. The bed was soft and the room quiet. I got a room with twin beds so I could sleep in a bed alone. I awoke early the next morning and headed to the condo. Crystal arrived on time.

"Hi," I said, greeting Crystal at the door.

"How was your night?" she asked.

"Long, I stayed till almost ten cleaning up. I got most of the upstairs done. I just gotta paint one more closet." She followed me into the kitchen as I talked. I stuck a list of things to do on the refrigerator. "I meant to go by the list yesterday, but I forgot it."

I crossed off a few things on the list. Crystal walked over to the fridge, and we went over what still had to be done. Crystal would finish painting the basement staircase. I would finish with the last closet in the third bedroom. And then we would meet on the first floor.

I would clean the downstairs bathroom and the pantry and touch up the paint in the living room, dining room, and stairway. It would be hard work. The pantry had to be cleaned and painted. All the shelves had to be removed and scrubbed.

Crystal would clean the stove, refrigerator, countertops, and cabinets and touch up the paint on the main wall in the kitchen. She was happy to have the job.

I also cleaned the bathrooms, which was disgusting.

Stress and anxiety kept me working. I couldn't rest. All I thought about was my condo, which led me to thinking about money, and that stressed me out. Something told me I was going broke, fast. I didn't know what to do. So I worked. And to me, cleaning was money. So I cleaned, fast, almost moving with superhuman speed.

For the first time, I thought about coming home after graduating from Western. As I cleaned the bathroom, I looked in the mirror and remembered the first time I'd looked in that mirror and realized it was mine. Slowly, the bathroom was my bathroom again. I looked around. It felt like home again.

I enjoyed talking to Crystal. We shared stories about our lives and talked about being mothers. I learned a lot from her. The most important lesson she taught me was that you should never let anyone steal your power or your joy.

I cleared my head, and regardless of how I felt, I kept motivated, focusing on the end in sight.

When we finished the working day, I was sad to see Crystal go. But her work with me was over. It was time for her to move on.

"Thank you for everything," I said as I walked Crystal to the door.

"Take care," she said.

Crystal and I hugged. I watched her leave. Then I went upstairs to relax before I went to Lowe's to by some new Venetian blinds for the living and dining room windows.

The next weekend, I returned to Lansing and did the same thing. Jonathan and I left Kalamazoo immediately after he got home from school; I didn't have a Friday class.

I arrived in Lansing Friday evening. I checked into my hotel room and dropped Jonathan off at my mom's house. I let Jonathan spend the night with mom because there wasn't that much work left and he would be in the way. I went to the condo and cleaned for a few hours and then went back to the hotel for the night.

Working in the condo was a bit lonely without Crystal. I hoped that I would see her again one day and that we would be friends. She may never know how much her presence changed my situation and my life.

I left for the condo early the next morning. I had to steam clean all the carpets, paint the downstairs closet, and wait for the trash and carpet companies. I wanted to get an early start.

Cleaning the condo was easy; fixing the repairs proved less so. Lowe's wanted nearly $400 to fix the basement door—an amount I couldn't afford to pay. The representative who came to give me an estimate told me that I could have the grate rebuilt for a cheaper price when he came to look at the door that Friday.

He looked around the condo and chuckled when he saw the mess. I pursed my lips and hung my head low. I then gave him a brief overview of what happened, leaving out the fact that one of the tenants was my brother.

He felt sorry for me. "You can go to a woodworking company; they can do the work for you," he told me.

At first I thought he was a prick for laughing at me; it turned out he was a cool guy.

I put the grate in my trunk and brought it back to Kalamazoo with me that Sunday night. Monday I found a woodworking company in Kalamazoo, Dawson Woods. The company specialized in cabinets, countertops, doors, and specialty woodwork.

Getting the grate fixed was not so easy. Dawson Woods wanted nearly $400 to rebuild the grate. I could tell by the displays of marble and granite lying around that Dawson would be expensive, but I'd never imagined the bid would be that high.

My heart sank, and disappointment showed in my eyes when the woodworker gave me the estimate. Seeing that I was about to cry, he gave me an idea.

"You can take the grate to Lowe's and have them cut you a piece the same size as the grate. Make sure you get a piece for the front of the door and one for the back. You can cut a hole for ventilation and screw a grate over it," he told me.

He was an old white man with crystal green eyes. I stared at him, looking into the iris of his eyeballs as he gave me instructions. I thanked him as he handed me the busted grate. "Good luck," he said, as I walked out the door.

The person who assisted me at Lowe's was great. I went over what the man at Dawson Woods had told me, and the Lowe's representative helped me find exactly what I needed. He cut two pieces of wood the size of the busted grate then he sold me two metal vents to place over the holes that I was to cut.

He gave me a helpful tip. "If you can't cut out the rectangle, drill a bunch of little holes in the area where the grate will go with a drill. That will work just as well. All you need is ventilation to let the air out," he explained.

I thanked him and headed to the front counter to check out.

The microwave was not as expensive to fix. I got the repair number printed inside the door and called Sears. When the repairman came, I was surprised to learn that in addition to having a busted handle, the microwave no longer worked. For $140, Sears replaced the handle and got the microwave running.

In the downstairs bathroom, I replaced the towel rack that had been ripped off the wall. I bought a replacement rack at Lowe's and installed it myself. It took some patching, painting, and manipulation, but the new rack worked well and looked professionally installed.

The same company that had installed the linoleum floor in the dining room replaced the carpet in the living room and the upstairs bedroom. I explained the situation with my condo, including and the numerous violations, to the carpet layer. He told me that the association was running a scam and that I should file paperwork with the courts to fight the violations. I would later regret not heeding his advice.

After Express Trash Removal had removed all the furniture, I learned that Green's dog had left stains in the carpet. I had no choice but to replace the basement carpet as well.

Replacing the basement carpet proved disastrous. I let my friend Trio talk me into hiring his uncle to do the work. "He a carpenter," Trio told me. "He fixes houses for a living."

Trio's uncle's price was cheap, and when he finished with the basement, I could see why. When I met Trio's uncle, I thought he looked lethargic and I considered telling him not to do my carpet, but I wanted to save money, and I didn't want to hurt Trio's feelings.

I replaced only the carpet on the staircase and a large section the dog had frequented the most.

The work was sloppy. Hundreds of staples showed on the staircase leading into the basement, and he cut and measured the carpet wrong. I was pissed, but I let it go. It looked good enough for Keydah to move in, and it had only cost me $250 for the carpet and labor. I was out of money, and I had no other choice but to accept the work as it was.

I decided that I would have the entire basement carpet replaced after Keydah moved out in a year. At the time, I had made up my mind to move back to Lansing after graduating from Western. Hopefully I would have my finances back in order by then.

My life became clear to me the night before I was to turn the condo over to Keydah. I left for Lansing at five o'clock. It was the last day of September, and the winter sun was setting. The sun had a strange, yellow glow, and Jonathan and I commented on the sky as we headed down the street.

I was extremely high off marijuana when I merged onto I-69 North. I had a felt like I was going to drive off the highway. Several times, I became scared, but I accelerated and focused.

Jonathan was in the passenger seat. I talked to him and listened to the radio to keep from thinking about crashing. But the thought was there, and it wouldn't go away. I felt as if my time had come, and I was going to fly off the highway.

I reached Charlotte, a small city twenty minutes outside of Lansing. Without warning, something large and brown leaped onto the highway running fast. It turned and looked at me with large, hollow eyes. The creature was the size of the entire front end of my car and as tall as the roof.

I was going seventy miles per hour. I couldn't slow down. I had two choices—hit the deer or swerve. Something told me to swerve, and so I obeyed.

I jerked the steering wheel hard to the left. I avoided the deer but began spinning down the highway. After the first spin, I began screaming.

On the second spin, I glanced at myself in the rearview, and for a moment I was no longer in the car. I was looking down at myself, and what I saw horrified me. I saw myself, mouth open screaming, eyes full of fear and terror. I no longer heard myself screaming, but I knew I was. I could see myself, and in the faint distance, I could hear my death approaching.

Jonathan put his Nintendo DS down and began screaming with me as we hit the fourth spin. Once again I looked in the rearview mirror. We were going backward off the highway and heading for a ditch. In my path, lay a large tree that had been broken in half and large, sharp splinters protruded from its broken trunk.

We were heading straight for the tree. I knew it. I was going to die, but at least I had my son with me. The thought of leaving him behind was and still is too much to bear. If I went, he had to come with me.

The tree spikes were long enough to bust the back windshield and reach us.

My Cadillac left the highway backward and headed down into the ditch, getting closer and closer to the tree trunk. Then my car stopped. I faced forward. I stared at the road ahead. No sound came from my throat. I wasn't sure what to do. I looked behind me. All I could see was shards of wood and debris and a forest of trees.

A car stopped, and three men got out.

"Are you okay?" one of the men asked me as I opened my door.

I fell into his arms and cried. Shaking, I shook my head no. "I thought I was going to die," I told him.

"I can't believe you made it. We saw the deer, and then all we saw were headlights spinning all around. I can't believe you didn't flip. We thought you were gonna flip."

We turned and looked at the tree. "I can't believe I didn't

crash into that tree. At the very least, I didn't think I was going to walk away from this," I said astonished.

Jonathan walked over to me crying. "Mom, let's go home," he said.

"No, baby. We gotta make it to Lansing."

The man looked at me. "Bless you," he said.

Still crying, I said," I'm glad that I was the only car and no one else was dragged in this with me."

I looked at my car. There was not a scratch; no insurance claim would be made—nothing.

I continued to cry and shake.

"You should call someone," the man suggested.

"Yeah, Mom. Call someone," Jonathan agreed.

.

I picked up the phone and called Trio. I don't know why, but that is what the spirit told me to do. I told him what happened. "God is trying to kill me," I concluded.

"Nova, go to church," he said softly.

I wasn't ready for his advice. I was afraid of church, and I knew it. I went sometimes but never all the way. I wasn't a full Christian. Technically, I had no religion, so I tried to avoid church whenever possible.

I continued to cry. "God is trying to kill me," I repeated. "You know what type of person I've been—especially lately. God is trying to kill me."

All that morning, all I'd thought about was how much I hated my family and how much I hated my life. I'd even wished that I had never been born. I believed that God had heard my thoughts and sent the deer as a punishment.

To be ungrateful is to commit one of the biggest sins. That morning, I had forgotten all of my blessings and only remembered the curses. In a sudden rush that I will never forget, I was reminded.

Trio tried to calm me down while one of the men called the

police. "You should wait here until the police come," the man said.

I took his advice. I wasn't ready to get back on the highway.

"See if the car starts," another one of the men suggested.

I climbed into my car and turned the key. The engine started with no problems. To shaken to drive myself out of the ditch, I asked one of the men. "Can you do it for me? Right now, I trust you more than I trust myself."

We switched places, and he easily drove my car up the ditch and onto the side of the highway. The five of us waited until the police arrived. Seeing that I had help, the men felt it was safe to go. I was sad to see them leave. I felt as if we had become friends.

Before he left, the first man to greet me walked over to me. He extended his hand to me, and I shook it. He looked me in the eyes, serious and focused, and said, "Thank you." Then the three men climbed back in his car, waved good-bye to the officers and me, and left.

I will never know why he thanked me. Perhaps I tought him something about life that he didn't know, maybe he had realized how precious life is as much as I did. All I know is that because of him I was able to hold myself together and make it out of that situation.

Since there had been no accident, the officer talked to me for a few moments and then left. I continued on to Lansing. I couldn't shake the eerie feeling for the rest of the night, and neither could Jonathan.

"Man, I can't believe we're still alive," he said.

"I know," I told him. "That was the scariest thing that has ever happened to me."

"It was crazy. I was playing my DS, and then we started to spin. And I continued playing my DS. And then you started to scream, and I put the DS down, and I started to scream too."

I let out a little laugh. "Yeah that's how it happened."

"You know what I shoulda said after the accident?" he asked, looking at me as if he had the perfect answer.

"No, what?"

"Life comes at you fast."

Jonathan and I exploded into laughter. "Yeah, you're right it does. Now I understand that commercial."

We continued to laugh, and I even shared his joke with friends when I told them the story.

Later on, I talked to Mom about what happened. "I don't think God was trying to kill you," she said. "If God wanted you dead, you would be dead. God stopped the car."

I believed her. It was then that I felt the evil spirit in my life. I felt as if a negative force was trying to destroy me. The force was bigger than my disability, GM, Green, my condo, Grey, or anything else. All the terrible things in my life were connected. I was meant to fail. I became afraid and depressed.

Two weeks after that, while driving home from campus, I had another deer experience. It was early in the morning, and few cars were on the road. I had to stop and wait because all the ducks in the pond decided to cross the street. The last duck was hurt, and so I had to wait extra long as it wobbled along.

After the ducks had crossed, I continued on. But as soon as I rounded the curve, I stopped. Three deer paced back and forth on the side of the road. I had a feeling that they would run out in front of me. I was right. Without warning, the mother deer dashed out in front of my car followed by two small deer.

Then it happened again. A few weeks later, as I was walking home from school, I spotted a large deer crossing the street. A few months after that, as I was waiting for the bus at the bus stop, I spotted a large deer walking across the street. After that, I began to hate deer.

The time to turn the apartment over came quickly. On October 1, I walked Keydah through my condo again. This time, it was clean with new carpet and fresh paint. Keydah couldn't hide her surprise. She brought her mother with her to the lease signing.

Her mother loved my condo and told me so. I liked her mother and got a good feeling about who I was giving my home to this time. I even got to meet her dad and brother when they came to help mover her in. I was still doing last-minute repairs on the closet door in one of the upstairs bedroom, and so I was still around when the movers came.

Keydah signed a year lease with me. I headed back to Kalamazoo, hopeful that my condo was in good hands. At the very least, Green was gone, and that made me feel better.

There was still one large issue to deal with—the citation violations. The violations kept coming even when my condo sat empty. After the last violation for loud noise in the parking lot, I called Buckthorn Management Company, who had now replaced Maplegrove Management Company.

Pissed, I let the representative handling Fairfield Condominium Association have a piece of my mind. I let her know that I thought the violations were racially motivated, and I wouldn't stand for discrimination.

"Come in and talk to the board directly," she told me over the phone.

I agreed to come to the next meeting, which was to be held that Tuesday. I met with the association for the first time the first week of November 2007.

I arrived at the clubhouse that Tuesday at exactly seven o'clock, the meeting time. I sat on the sofa, listening to the affairs of the association and realized that, although Fairfield had hundreds of occupants, only two other people besides me and the board members were at the meeting.

It's not a good thing that no one comes to the meetings. No one being here gives the board a lot of power and control over what happens out here. I need to start coming to these meetings. When I move back, I'ma make sure I go to the meetings.

I patiently waited on one of the sofas lined up against the wall until the meeting had ended. Then it was time to discuss my situation. I sat down at the long table across from the board members and a representative from Buckthorne and stated my case. I smiled at them and tried to be friendly. "I'm here to discuss the violations and the fact that I kept receiving citations for my condo, even when no one lived there," I said.

I sat across from the six white women, angry and trying to control myself. Each met my explanation with a somber stare. Immediately, I didn't like them.

"We have been trying to get in contact with you. We didn't have your address," a woman with straight, shoulder-length hair told me.

"I moved. I had my mail forwarded with the post office. Even if you didn't have my address, I should have still received the citations."

"We've sent several letters and even had our private investigator serve your brother with a notice, but he refused to give us your address," she said.

"I've talked to my brother several times, and he denies such allegations. Even so, you don't have any proof of the allegations to begin with."

"We have witnesses," she said.

"Why didn't anyone call the police?" I asked.

"We were afraid of gang retaliation. There looked to be drug activity going on at the house, and we were afraid. Cars would pull up. People would go in, stay twenty minutes, and come out. This went on all night."

We discussed the other violations; the lease and rental agreement violations would be overturned, but nothing else. They were adamant in their claim of the drug and gang activity, and they wanted all $10,000.

I still wasn't convinced. With no evidence, I didn't feel I should pay them $10,000. Another woman with short, curly hair chimed in with a story that was supposed to prove to me the dangers that my brother and his roommates brought to Fairfield.

"I was out walking my dog, and one of the guys let his dog out to use the bathroom," she said. "Then he started walking away. I said to him, 'Hey pick that up.' He just looked at me, laughed, and walked away. I told him that I was a member of the board. He didn't care."

The woman was still angry as she told her story. She seemed to be taking her frustrations out on me. I listened to what she had to say. It was true that she had been treated with disrespect, but that didn't make my brother and his roommates drug dealers.

But I knew better. I never told the board members about what happened with my condo. Still, that didn't make me guilty, and I didn't believe that I should pay $10,000 for loud noise and shitting dogs.

I argued with them for nearly an hour. "We'll look over the information and get back to you," the association president told me.

I headed back to Kalamazoo that night, angrier than ever before. I hated Green and the association.

I went to talk to Jenny again. We had a lengthy discussion about my brother and family. Jenny's double chin wobbled as she talked. Her toes looked as if they wanted to bust out of her cheap shoes. She explained to me that my situation was common.

"Your family has grown bitter and jealous of you because you're trying to better yourself and they're not. That's how my dad's side of the family is. They stared treating me the same way once I became a lawyer. My dad's side is poor, and they're unwilling to work to change their lives. They took their anger out on me because I was trying to better myself."

Jenny suggested that I sue Green for the whole $10,000 plus the damages to my condo. Knowing that, even with an order from the judge to garnish his wages, Green was uncollectible, I decided not to pursue that route. I had a better idea.

Topaz had suggested that I take Green on a reality court show. "If you win your case, the show pays you," she told me.

Enthused, I googled Judge Joe Brown and Judge Mathis and sent them both an e-mail. Someone from Judge Joe Brown's show contacted me the next day.

CHAPTER THIRTEEN:
Meet the Producer

In September 2007, I spoke with Myra Rich, an assistant producer for the Judge Joe Brown's show. Myra confirmed that, if I won my settlement, the show would pay for the amount of the settlement within thirty days of my court appearance.

I told her that my situation was desperate and needed to be put in the next round of taping.

"I'll talk to my supervisor and see what I can do," she said.

Myra explained the process to me. First, I had to go file the case in Lansing's civil court. As soon as I had my case number, I was to contact her again. From there, the show would take over my case.

If Green decided not to do the show, I could still sue him in Lansing. That was my backup plan. I figured that Green would do the show rather than face a $10,000 lawsuit.

I learned that the case would be dismissed once we were on the show, as well as all fines and fees.

I didn't discuss my plans with anyone in the family, except my mom who was beyond thrilled with the possibility that Green and I might be on television.

"This is a good thing. It's not like the two of you are going on TV for something bad like a baby. You guys are talking about property and a condo. That's respectable," Mom told me.

I became enraged at her comment. "You think this is a good thing? Green trashed my condo and left me with a ten thousand dollar-bill. It ain't for a good reason that we're going on TV," I said.

I didn't bother to argue with her beyond that. I knew how Mom was. She didn't think like a regular person. Any other parent would have been concerned about what was happening, but not Mom. She was excited. "My kids are going on national television," she said over and over again.

I stayed out of contact with the rest of the family. I was still not speaking to Asia because of her insensitive comment when I called her crying about my condo being trashed.

I was tired of Asia. She made sure that she played the supporting role to all of her friends, but whenever I needed her, all she did was ridicule me. I didn't need her giving me her two cents. Besides, Asia had been trying to get on TV for years. I had a feeling that she would be jealous and do nothing but hate on me.

I tried not to talk about the lawsuit with Jonathan because I knew it made him upset. Back in Kalamazoo, we continued on with life as if Lansing had never happened. Jonathan rarely commented on the situation. If he said anything at all, it was something like, "That's messed up that Green trashed our condo."

Jonathan had turned ten on the June 14. He was old enough to understand the divide in the family. To keep him sheltered, though, I saved my rants for other people.

I talked to my friends in Kalamazoo about my problems with my family when they came over to visit, but they weren't really there for me. So I tried my best to keep my worries to myself.

What I learned is that the only friend a person has is God. For the most part my situation was something that my "friends" could talk about to their other friends when I wasn't around. Looking back, I would realize that not one person gave me advice on how to let the bad blood between Green and me go and move on. No one told me that I was wrong for hating my brother. They simply stared at me and waited for me to continue.

My only pleasure was writing.

That fall semester, I started my third book. It was my best book so far. I called it *Soul Mourning*. I decided that, after I graduated, I would focus on getting it published.

I still had my first book hidden on the top shelf of my closet. I could have continued to work on it, but I decided that the book needed a lot of work and I was better of starting over, using all the knowledge I'd gained from the English department.

I filed my court case with the Lansing court in September. After three weeks of waiting for my case number, I called the court.

"You already have your case number," the receptionist told me. "It's the number on the top of your docket."

She guided me to a series of numbers on top of the court papers.

Ecstatic, I hung up and immediately sent Myra an e-mail with my case number.

Originally, I'd planned to sue Green for the entire $10,000. A few days after I sent her my case number, Myra called me with bad news. I had to drop my civil case in Lansing and file a case in small claims court because the show only handled small claims cases. That meant that I could only sue for $5,000.

I was disappointed, but I still moved forward as directed.

I had to drive back to Lansing and drop the case in one court and file another case in another court. But I didn't care. I would do whatever it took to get my money.

Once in Lansing, I learned more bad news. Because of Michigan law, I could only sue Green for up to $3,000 in small claims. I was disheartened, but I pressed forward.

"I still want to do the show," I told Myra. "Three thousand dollars is better than nothing. And I know Green doesn't have a dime to pay me."

The show had me running back and forth almost every day, gathering and sending documents. In preparation for the show, Myra directed me to send her all of my case information. I had to gather all my receipts, pictures, and any other information I had. In true Hollywood style, Myra even sent DHS to personally pick up the information from me.

There were several disclaimers I had to fill out. I signed a form stating that I had never participated in a reality court show, that I was not an actress, and that I would wait at least a year before I went on another reality court show. I even had to fill out a questionnaire that asked me all about myself, my future goals, and current occupation.

I explained that I was a disabled GM employee and a college student who wanted to write books for a living. I gave the show ample information about myself and, when asked, I told them all about my family. I wasn't ashamed of my past; to me, it was what had made me.

It was through e-mailing Myra that I began to understand myself. I liked to talk about my private life. I realized that I had a big mouth because I told her anything she wanted to know, and I answered all her questions honestly.

Myra made me feel as if someone truly cared. I loved e-mailing her. She always responded right away. I was open and honest with Myra. I had nothing to hide. I even told her about the drug and gang allegations. At a time when I had distanced myself from most people, I found my e-mail conversations with her soothing.

Myra's life was somewhat like mine. Her mother had suffered from nervous breakdowns because of General Motors too. She paid special attention to my story and gave supportive advice. "I hope your mom is recovering well," Myra e-mailed me.

"No, she's not. No one wants to be bothered with her since she had her stroke. No one wants to take care of her, even though my entire family lives around the corner from her and one of my brothers even lives in the same house with her," I responded back.

"I'm sorry to hear that."

"So am I."

During that time, I tried to force the hate and anger toward Green out of my mind, even though I thought about him daily; I thought about the violations and the fact that he had stolen $500 from me the last time I'd seen him.

I began imagining myself stabbing Green in the throat. I wanted to kill him. Sometimes, the thought consoled me; other times, it frightened me. Whenever my fantasy got out of hand, I reminded myself that I would not see Green because I was away at college. There was safety in distance. I understood that.

Besides that, I prayed. I understood that anger was a normal response and that most people in my situation would feel the same way. Day and night, I prayed that I wouldn't lose it and hurt someone. It worked, and as time went on, I was able to deal with the situation.

One thing kept me going—the bus rides to campus. I lived around the corner from WMU. As I rode the bus each day, that felt peaceful. I felt connected to my school. I loved walking to the bus stop, even in the rain or snow.

The bus rides were a humbling experience. Even though I drove a Cadillac, I still didn't feel to self-important to get on the bus. That's how I knew I was human. I was willing to lower myself, change, and adapt, all for a shot at my dream.

On the bus, I got to know my fellow students. I watched them, listened to them, and learned from them. I realized that I wasn't the only one who was poor and struggling to make it through college. On the bus, I never forgot why I had come to Kalamazoo. I never forgot that I was a college student.

Catching the bus meant that I had to leave home at a certain time and plan my day around the bus schedule. Doing that helped ensure that I was always on time for class. I lived so close that, if I missed the bus, I simply walked.

Two days before the show on December 7, I went to the mall and bought something special to wear just for the show. My friend, Vernon, and Jonathan went shopping with me. Myra discussed with me what looked good on camera and what did not. I tried to stay away from white, as it made everything seem to blend together.

I chose a tan button-down with soft gold stripes and a pair of casual khakis. I stepped out of the Express dressing room, looked at Jonathan, and Vernon and said, "This is the outfit I'm gonna sue my brother in."

Jonathan smiled and shook his head at me. Vernon did the

same. I laughed and went back in the dressing room to change back into my clothes.

I wore my hair pulled back and dyed jet black with a full bundle of super long, soft and wavy hair wrapped around the ponytail. The hair reached down to almost the middle of my back. The accent jewelry I picked out pulled everything together and brought out the gold in the shirt. No matter how I felt, I knew I looked good.

The night before I left, I tried to push all thoughts of what was to happen out of my mind. Vernon got on my nerves by telling me about myself.

"You're a drama queen," he told me.

I looked at him. "What? What the fuck are you talking about? I'm not a drama queen. My brother trashed my condo and left me with a ten thousand dollar-bill. Now I'm gonna sue him. It's just business."

"Yeah, you're gonna sue him on Judge Joe Brown." Vernon looked over at me with sarcasm in his voice and said, "They're gonna love you in Hollywood."

I ignored Vernon. What did he know? The situation wasn't his. If he had to go through my experience, perhaps he would do the same thing. Or maybe he wouldn't. Not everyone was strong enough to endure and complete his or her mission at all costs.

Vernon and I talked some more about LA. He was concerned that I was going alone.

"Don't worry," I told him. "All I'm going to do is go to the airport, go to the show, and take a walk downtown during the day. I'm staying at the Sheraton downtown; that's a nice hotel. What's the worst that could happen to me? I'm not bringing any weed with me. I'll be fine."

I knew how to be smart. My plan was to stay focused, not talk to any strangers, and avoid going adrift. If I did that, I would be okay.

CHAPTER FOURTEEN:
Showtime

I WOULD BE IN LA for three days and two nights. As it was my first time in LA, I decided to enjoy myself and forget about Green. Despite the circumstances surrounding my trip, I still wanted to have a good time and see some sights.

I hugged Jonathan extra tight before I left him with my mom.

"I hope you win your case," he told me.

"I will. Green doesn't have a case. All the evidence is against him," I said.

Mom laughed.

"Earnest and Green was downstairs going over his defense. Earnest was like, 'Tell them this. Make sure you say that,'" she told me.

I looked at her. "The only thing Green should be going over is his apology."

I expected the show to expiate my losses. That was the only reason I remained calm once I'd heard that Earnest was advising Green. Pissed, I left Mom's house feeling as if I had been betrayed.

I arrived at the Lansing Airport thirty minutes early, but my flight left two hours late due to problems with the airplane.

I arrived in Chicago two hours behind schedule. I was a bit upset because of the delay, so I occupied myself by thinking about Los Angeles. I wondered what it would look like in real life, what the weather and people would be like.

After an hour of waiting, we were able to board the plane. I made it to my seat and sat down next to a white woman. Soon, we began a conversation. She was different, and I was entranced by her. I found out that she was from Europe originally, and that especially sparked my attention.

I never told her why I was going to LA because she never asked. She wanted to talk, and so I listened.

"I live in Orange County," she told me for the third time.

I looked at her, not understanding what was so great about Orange County. There must have been something special about Orange County because she very much wanted me to know that she lived there.

"What's the difference? I asked looking confused.

"Orange County is the suburb."

I understood then. Suburb life was great. My condo was suburb life.

She told me what it was like for her and her husband when they first came to America and started their new life. I thought her story was interesting. She told me tales her life in Europe. I was impressed I then hoped that I would be able to make it out of my situation.

I looked at her sadly. "I hope I can make it after I graduate."

"Why wouldn't you be able to make it?" she asked.

She would never know my life. She would never understand the plight of a black woman. And so I stared at her silently.

After a few seconds, a slight smile appeared on her face. She knew my answer, and so I never responded.

Because I'm black. It was easy for you and your husband to come here and get set up because you're white. White people stick together. Black people don't.

I turned and looked at her. We stared at each other. I noticed the designer bag at her feet and her slightly tanned skin. I could tell that she worked out at a gym.

As we continued talking, I thought some more.

Well, just because I'm black don't mean I can't make it in the world. I'm smart. I have an education. I'm pretty.

I turned to the woman and gave her an answer so honest I

didn't I felt that way until it came out. "I don't know where to go," I said. It was true.

I was lost. After college, I had no destination. I had no man, no money, and a son to take care of. I was afraid. The world seemed so big.

She smiled at me and nodded her head, happy that I had figured it out. *Because I'm black* was no real answer, and she knew it. So did I.

After an hour of waiting on the plane, we had to disembark. This was now my second delay. Still not over the first delay in Michigan I became frustrated and angry. The plane had serious mechanical problems. At first, the motor in the windshield wiper had given out. After fixing that, the mechanics learned that the entire engine had to be replaced.

A voice came over the intercom. "Don't worry, folks, we'll get you to LA tonight, even if that means grabbing another plane," the pilot announced.

Pissed, I got off the plane and sat in the lobby. After another three hours of waiting, the airport closed, and United Airlines announced that they were putting everyone up in a hotel room for the night and then flying us out in the morning.

I left my seat in the lobby, walked up to the receptionist, and began complaining. I complained and complained until I had nothing left to say.

Because I'd argued with the flight attendants, I was pushed to the back of the rebooking line. I didn't get a flight out of Chicago until 12:00 p.m. the next day. I was furious. I called Myra. Frantic, we tried to come up with another plan, but there was none. Foolishly, I stayed with flight 201 instead of catching another flight to LA.

On the bus ride to the hotel, all the passengers, including me, swapped stories about why they were going to LA. Everyone listened to me because I ranted about being stuck in Chicago the most. I talked about the complaint letter I planned to write to the airline officials.

I met a group of people who were on their way to Australia and another woman who was going to LA for an important job interview. I quickly became the center of attention when I explained my reason for going to LA. I didn't care. I told my fellow passengers about my brother and our court appearance. I shocked even myself at how comfortable I felt talking about my personal drama with complete strangers.

Even in the check-in line at the Holiday Inn, I continued to trash Green. I had everyone laughing, yet I wanted to stop. I felt like family matters should be personal but the situation with Green had become a public spectacle and I wanted everyone to know my side of the story.

A little girl with her mother looked at me with sad blue eyes and said, "That's your brother."

"Uh-huh," I said, turning away.

She tugged my arm and kept looking at me sadly. "But that's your brother," she said again.

I looked at her and smiled. "Don't worry, little girl," I said. "Justice will be served."

The other adults and I laughed.

"Oh you," her mother said, as they stepped to the counter to be checked into their hotel for the night.

The woman who was going to LA for a job interview turned out to be nice. Sympathetic to my story, she offered to try and get me on an earlier flight out of Chicago. She was booked on the 7:00 a.m. flight and a nine o'clock flight. If all else failed, I would take her nine o'clock. Still, she wanted to try and get me a seat on the seven o'clock flight.

"If I get there after nine they're gonna let me get dressed at the studio," I told her.

She shook her head no and said, "That's a public place. You don't wanna get dressed in a public place. You wanna get dressed at your room."

I agreed. LA was still four hours behind Chicago time and that gave me leeway. I figured that no matter what time I arrived in LA it was best for me to get dressed in private.

We chatted for a while. I learned that she traveled a lot for work. She was interviewing for a top position with a pharmaceutical company. I learned a lot from her in a short time. We talked about school. "Education is how they weed us out," she told me.

She looked biracial. I never thought that a biracial person could connect to my life. I'm black, and she was half white. At that moment, it all made sense. We were the same.

I'd always wanted a traveling job. I'd wanted to fly every day—hitting two maybe three cities a day. But after talking to my new friend, I realized a job like that wasn't all it was made out to be.

I met my new friend in the lobby at 5:00 a.m., having slept for no more than three hours. Her plan worked, and I was on the first flight out of Chicago. I fell asleep on the plane, and when I awoke, I was in a new world. Sunny skies and palm trees greeted me, even in December. I took my coat off and enjoyed the sunshine.

The cab driver who took me from the airport to the hotel was great. I told him where I was from.

"Lansing, huh," he said with a thick Middle Eastern accent. "And do you know who's my most favorite person in the whole world from Lansing?"

He slowed his cab down as if he would kick me out if I didn't know. But I did know the answer. Who is everyone's most favorite person from Lansing, Michigan? We all know him.

"Magic Johnson," I exclaimed, nearly jumping out my seat.

I loved Magic Johnson. He'd made Lansing proud. He was an inspiration to people from Lansing who wanted to get out and make something of themselves but thought they couldn't because they were from Lansing. Lansing was on the map because of Magic Johnson. Despite his situation, he'd continued to press forward. May the Lord always bless Magic Johnson.

I dressed quickly at the hotel and arrived at NBC studio on Sunset Boulevard in full makeup.

"Do you have any cameras or camera phones?" a man in charge of check-in asked.

I handed him my camera phone, and he checked my name off a list. I was led into a small room with three other people and a television set playing reruns of Judge Joe Brown. In the room with me were a black girl who was suing her sister over a car and a middle-aged couple from California. The couple was suing an antique toy dealer over a fake Hot Wheels truck.

The four of us openly discussed our cases. I noticed that the black girl took special care to say sweet things about her sister and their relationship. I didn't follow this pattern. I talked about how much I hated my brother. Still pissed about him trashing my condo, I talked about that too. I noticed the black girl giving me a crazy look, so I gave her one back.

I turned from her and began talking with the married couple. They were friendly. The woman was worried because the man they were suing still hadn't shown up. She went over her case while she waited. The man had apparently offered a thirty-day return policy, and they had returned the truck within the thirty days.

I had some advice to offer them. "It doesn't matter if the toy was a fake or not. You returned the car within the thirty days, so you should win your case just off that. Just tell the judge that you complied with the return policy, and you should be fine," I advised.

The woman turned to her husband with excitement in her eyes. "Did you hear that? She's right. We did return the car within the return period."

The couple was excited to have a new angle from which to plead their case.

Lucy, the executive producer, and Myra came to get me. "She's eating," Lucy said, once she saw me.

Her comment annoyed me, but I let it slide. I wanted to be nice to the people connected to the show.

Lucy looked me over. "You're beautiful," she said with an almost dazed look.

I understood the look she gave me. Pretty people got better ratings. I wiped the crumbs from my hand and stood up to shake her hand.

I was estatic to see Myra in person. I felt as if she was an old friend. I was comfortable around her. I noticed how pretty she was. Petite, well dressed with long auburn hair she exuded a strong presence in the small waiting room.

I observed Lucy as well. A few years older than Myra she had a mature look. She wore a short, snazzy haircut and sharp clothes. She had soft brown eyes and I could tell that she took care of herself well.

We sat in a small, private room and discussed my case. We compared files—the one that I sent to them and the original paperwork, which I'd been reminded to bring.

"What is this?" Lucy asked me. She held up an old listing of my condo.

"Oh, that's just the for-sale listing. I forgot it was in there."

The picture was a perfect snapshot of my old life.

"Is this what it looked like when you lived there?"

"Yeah, that's all my stuff," I said, trying to remain humble.

At that moment, I wondered if moving to Kalamazoo had been a good idea in the first place.

"This place is gorgeous. Why did you let your brother move in here?" Lucy shot me a look. "Kids don't live in a place like this."

There was nothing I could say to refute her point. She was right. Kids did not live in a place like that. If it wasn't for my job at General Motors, I wouldn't have lived in a place like that either.

We finished going through my file and then I went for makeup. Since my makeup was already done, the makeup artist brushed me with powder and sent me back to the waiting room.

A tall, white girl came into the waiting room to talk to me. She was pretty, just like Myra and Lucy. It was then that I realized that everyone at the show was attractive. The girl brought some forms for me to sign—paperwork for tax purposes. We chitchatted for a moment. I still had nothing nice to say about Green, and that pissed her off. For the first time in my life, I got the "Hollywood stare."

The girl stared at me with cold, hazel eyes. For a long time she remained silent. We looked at each other, saying nothing. I was pissed that she had taken Green's side.

An edge to one of the documents in my file had been bent. I wanted to reach over and straighten it out. The girl knew it too. She looked at the paper and then at me and then back at the paper. I watched her for a while. Then I looked down at the paper and then back at her. I didn't reach over and fix the small crinkle like I wanted to. I kept my eyes locked on her.

It was then that I developed my own Hollywood stare. The Hollywood stare would come in handy during my journalist days at the school newspaper and during my fight with the condo association.

Lucy and Myra came to get me and moved me to another room. Now was my chance to ask Lucy more about the process.

"Does Green have to pay the show back?" I asked her.

"No. After this, everything is done. Nothing is on his credit." Lucy looked at me. "If there was nothing in it for the other side, no one would come out here."

I nodded, trying to shake off my disappointment. We then left for the other room.

We were alone in the other room. It was time to discuss my lead—what I would say before I went into the courtroom. The lead would be played to television viewers before they saw my case.

After some back and forth, we came up with a line. I was to say, "My brother is a liar. He trashed my condo." I felt comfortable with my line. It was short and catchy.

"What's Green's line?" I asked.

"His line is, 'It's her condo; it's her responsibility,'" Lucy told me.

"Who thought of that?" I asked, looking back and forth from Myra to Lucy.

"I did," Lucy said, almost guiltily.

Lucy knew she was sending Green out there with a bad line and a terrible defense. But I didn't feel sorry for Green. During his confab with Earnest, he'd planned his defense. All Green cared about was being on TV, and so if he was made a fool, it was his own fault.

I tried not to let my hurt show after she read his line. After all that Green had done to me, he was not sorry; in fact, he was happy. At that moment, all doubt that Green might have some good character left in him evaporated from my mind.

"This is for you. Go have yourself a steak dinner tonight," Lucy said.

She placed seventy dollars in cash on the coffee table in front of me. Wordlessly, I picked the money up, nodded, and placed the cash in my purse.

Lucy and Myra left the room again. The next time I was called, it was time for court. The sound technician fitted me with a microphone. He was a friendly man with an outgoing personality. I felt relaxed around him and tried not to think about what I was about to do.

The set was nothing like I had imagined. It looked like an unfinished room with open space and unpainted drywall. One wall had been fitted with windows, so I could see inside the courtroom. The studio audience was there. Lucky and Myra came out to meet me once more.

"Okay," Lucy said. "We're going to do your lead."

She led me down a short hall that led to an open space. The space had been decorated and painted. No one would know that everything around this space was patched drywall and cement flooring. "Do you remember your line?" she asked.

"Yes—My brother is a liar. He trashed my condo."

"Great. Just keep your eyes on Myra when you talk," Lucy

instructed. "When you're done, come back down that hall." She pointed to the hall we had just walked down.

I nodded. Myra faced me. The cameraman stood off at an angle. I turned to Myra, sincere and steady. I said my line. "My brother is a liar. He trashed my condo." The words came out clear and strong.

"Got it," the cameraman said.

I walked back down the hall and joined Lucy. When she saw me, she was surprised. "That was fast," she said. "We got us a one-liner here."

Lucy smiled and ushered me to my spot behind the window overlooking the courtroom. I could see Judge Joe Brown, and suddenly everything began to feel surreal yet real at the same time. For the first time since googling the show, I felt nervous.

"You know, I just was over there talking to your brother. When he saw all the lights and the set, he was smiling and shaking his head up and down. He said that he could get used to this," Lucy said. She folded her arms and shook her head.

Myra joined us and stood quietly.

"He said what!" I exclaimed. Hearing about Green's happiness sent me into a rage.

"I know. I couldn't believe it. After all that he has done to you, he's happy to be on TV. This whole thing is nothing more than a debut to him." Lucy seemed outraged.

"I knew it. My mom said that he was jumping up and down when he got the call. He was so excited to do the show that's all he's been thinking about. I can't wait to get out there." I stared at the courtroom. "I'm not gonna go Jerry Springer on him and disrespect your show, but I'm going off."

"Did you hear what she said?" Lucy asked, laughing. "She said Jerry Springer."

Lucy looked as if she wanted to give Myra a hug. Myra remained quiet. She had met Green too. I could tell that she liked him and wasn't okay with what was about to happen. But it wasn't her show.

Lucy loved drama. I smiled, ready to give it to her. Lucy had told me about Green at the last minute on purpose. She wanted me to erupt.

"Okay. Now when you get out there, just relax," Lucy said. "Start off with the introduction you practiced and then go on into your story. Now, the judge is his own person. I can't guarantee which way he's going to go. But you just tell him your story, and you'll be fine. Don't worry. Sometimes the judge starts to talk and doesn't stop. If that happens, just interrupt him. Ignore the studio audience behind you. They're paid."

She shot me a knowing glance, and I nodded.

"You'll be in court for about twenty or thirty minutes, even though only fifteen minutes will be aired. You're gonna do great. Remember, this is your moment. This is your show. You're brother trashed your condo and left you with a ten thousand dollar-bill. This is your chance to confront him."

"Okay," I said, ready for Green.

On the signal, I headed through the double doors. I entered the courtroom and locked eyes with Judge Joe Brown; he was the first to look away. Green came into the courtroom and walked over to his podium next to mine. I refused to look at him.

This is crazy. I can't believe I'm on Judge Joe Brown's show suing Green. I just can't believe it, I thought as I placed my file in front of me.

The worst part was the lights, which were hot and plentiful. Six cameras sat positioned on the ceiling behind Judge Joe Brown, and two cameramen were on the ground—one for me and one for Green. I did not count the cameras behind me. I was not allowed to turn around.

The judge began by asking me what happened. As planned, I began my story. "I got a call from my mom. She said, 'Nova, the police are looking for you.' I said, 'The police, why?' She said that they had a letter to give to me. She gave me the number, and I called the police department ..."

"Tell me about the loud noise," Judge Joe Brown interrupted.

"That came later," I said, continuing my story. "The officer said that he had a letter to send to me. After he sent me the letter, I called Fairfield Place, and they told me that they had an eviction notice for my brother and his two roommates."

"Tell me about the dogs," Judge Joe Brown interrupted again, trying to skip parts.

I looked him in the eye and I tried to relax. "That came later as well," I said. I resumed my story. "When I talked to the condo association, they told me that the eviction was due to excessive violations."

The judge looked at me for a moment, realizing that I was determined to tell the story my way. Showing me who had the final say, he cut me off, "I'ma get back to you later. You seem to have your story together. Now, let's get over to your brother," he said. "Son, what was you thinking!"

"Let's see, what was I thinking?" Green repeated, cynical and sarcastic.

This angered the judge, and he immediately attacked.

"Now, you're unemployed," the judge began.

"I'm not unemployed. I have a job," Green informed him.

"You do? Well tell me, son, what do you do?"

"I'm a telemarketer."

Please, Mom told me you just got fired for not going to work.

I kept the information to myself because I didn't want to further embarrass Green.

Judge Joe Brown pulled up a list of the violations. He pointed to the first one. "Loud noise and excessive traffic," he said. "Son, why didn't you turn your music down?"

Green answered, "We weren't being loud. Some people have their own level of discomfort. I had a good relationship with my neighbor. If she had a problem with the music, all she had to do was knock on the door and tell me to turn it down."

The judge rolled his eyes. "How many times did she have to tell you to turn the music down?"

"Not that many," Green responded.

That only angered the judge more. "Not that many? She should have only had to tell you once."

He stood up and began pacing back and forth. The judge continued to question Green about his actions.

Green had no real explanation for what had gone on in my condo. "She wasn't being professional. She didn't read the lease to me. I wasn't aware of what was in the lease," Green said.

I wasn't being professional? I thought. *Okay so I cussed you out a few times. Other than that, I was nothing but professional.*

I remained quiet. I didn't want to talk about the time when I cussed Green out. I knew Green wanted to talk about it, so I let his comment slide.

Judge Joe Brown wasn't buying it. "Now, your sister let you move into her condo, and this is what you do to her? And you see what your defense is. She should have told me. She didn't read the lease to me. You say you're a man, but you want your sister to take care of you."

That's right. Green's excuse is bullshit. Ain't nobody got time to read a damn lease to him. He don't need a lease to tell him to act right.

I halfheartedly listened to Judge Joe Brown's rant because I was somewhat pissed that I was not getting my Jerry Springer moment; I stopped paying attention. The lights were hot, and I was scared and nervous. I began thinking that I was going to have a nervous breakdown. I'm not sure where the thought came from, but once it was there, it didn't leave. That worried me. I wished I was high.

The judge began telling us a story about his own condo association. One time, some young hood boys were being loud and disruptive and terrorizing the neighbors. The association security wanted to call the police; Judge Joe Brown said no. He wanted to handle it himself.

"I'm a man," the judge said. "I'm not gonna run from some young boys. After I talked to them, I had them running out of there. You see, those boys needed some man training. Because of the lack of strong black men in the community, most young black men today don't know anything about being a man. They need man training. And that's what you're gonna get today, young man—some man training."

I knew that man training was a dig at our dad because any real father would have intervened in the condo situation. I loved it. I couldn't wait for the show to air so our dad could see and hear what a failure he had been.

The judge told Green that he was a representation of the fatherless generation of black men today. Green's actions in my condo proved that he was just another young thug. It was a disgrace to see a young, black mother trying to make it, and her thug brother comes along and tears her down.

"We need men in our community," the judge said.

I agreed. "Yes," I shouted out.

Green was pathetic. He tried to get laughs from the audience with smart comments and instead came across sounding ignorant. It was as if it had never dawned on him that he was wrong.

I was glad that the judge was letting Green have it, yet I wanted to be the one telling him how wrong he'd been. I wanted to be the one to make Green look stupid. I tried to tell the judge about the dogs, "He brought another dog into the condo after he had already gotten the first dog taken away."

Judge Joe Brown cut me off and began going off on Green about the dogs himself. "Why would you bring another dog into the condo if they already took the first dog away?" The judge stared at Green. "Why didn't you clean up after the dogs?"

"We did clean up after the dogs. Other people had dogs out there, and they weren't cleaning up after them," Green tried to explain.

The judge wasn't buying it. "It didn't matter what other people were doing. You needed to take responsibility for yourself."

Then the judge moved onto the gang and drug allegations. The more I listened, the more he began to sound like the condo association.

I decided to challenge his opinion. "Can I …" I began to ask a question.

The judge ignored me.

Flustered, I took a deep breath and exhaled. The floor cameraman next to me took a step closer and zoomed in on my face. It was then that I knew how difficult television could be. I tried again. "Can I ask you a question?"

Judge Joe Brown continued to ignore me.

I went for it any way, "Why are they drug dealers because they're black?" I asked.

He ignored me again. But as soon as I heard the studio audience, I knew I'd been heard. I decided from then on to interrupt whenever necessary.

Every time, I infused my opinion into the conversation, the judge ignored me. Finally he told me, "Be quiet because you don't know where I'm going with my story."

I realized that man training referred to me too.

Suddenly, Judge Joe Brown had more questions for me, "Are there association fees that you have to pay?" he asked.

"Yes."

"Now," he looked at me, "Were you relying on your brother to pay those association charges too?"

I sensed where he was heading. I stopped him before he could try and make that point. "No, I paid my association fees, and I paid my mortgage as well. And in the month of October, I had a successful turnover, and I turned my condo back to its original condition. I have a new renter now, and everything is fine."

If I would have said yes, then I was a typical hood chick relying on a drug dealer for financial support. I was proud that "no" was the honest answer.

The judge smiled. "So you held it together, and your brother slipped?"

"Yes," I said, glad that he understood.

The judge turned his attention back to Green. "You see, son. They want you to do this. They want you to drop out of school, sell drugs, and go to prison. That way you're not able to compete out here. The more young black men in prison, the less competition there is."

I listened closely. I'd never heard it put that way before, but it was like the woman on the plane told me. They weed us out with education. And they like it when we destroy ourselves because that means less completion in the job market, housing market, and school districts. And who were "they"? Everyone who's trying to get ahead. The less black people around, the easier it was for everyone else. It was the same for single moms. Most girls had to quit school when they had a baby, making it easier for the competition to get ahead.

"Let me ask you a question," Judge Joe Brown said to me.

"Sure," I said, ready for whatever.

"You're walking down a dark street in the middle of the night, and four black men are coming toward you. Would you be scared?"

A smile crept at the corner of my mouth halfway through his question. Every woman knows the answer to that. "I would be afraid if they were white," I said.

This time the studio audience remained silent, except for one woman behind me who let out an "uh."

I followed the voice. Casually I turned around to see who had responded to my comment. A black woman who looked to me in her early thirties exchanged glances with me and I knew it was her. From the look she gave me I could tell that she might agree.

I was not being mean; I simply wanted to show the judge and anyone else watching that crime wasn't racial. If I could have gained better control over my nerves, I would have said more.

Judge Joe Brown glanced back over at me. He seemed to have one more test for me.

In the waiting room, Myra had asked me about being a

teenage mother. Never tested on that subject before, I'd shown my weakness. As soon as Myra asked me, I began dissing Jonathan's father and complaining about my single-mom situation. The look Myra gave me let me know that, if I was to ever make it, I would have to get over Jonathan's father. I expected Judge Joe Brown to bring it up. Instead he went after Green.

"So you have a one-year-old son. You're already falling into the life," the judge said.

Green recoiled as if he was stung. "Whoa," he leaned back. "What do you mean I'm falling into the life?"

"You have a son. What kind of an example are you to him? What are you going to teach your son?" Judge Joe Brown asked.

I began making a series of faces as I prepared to interrupt again. I wanted to let Judge Joe Brown know that Green's maybe baby did not make him as a father. Sensing that I had something else to say, Judge Joe Brown asked me another question.

"You didn't know that he had a son, did you?" he said, half smiling.

"He has a son?"

"Don't ask me; ask him."

"I don't talk to him," I said, pointing my thumb in Green's direction.

"Ask him."

I turned and faced Green. "You have a son?" I asked, sounding surprised.

I guess the tone of my voice must have been comical because the studio audience laughed.

"You haven't talked to me in a while," Green said. He had a stupid look on his face. I guess he figured that this was going to be our moment, but I continued to look at him keeping my face straight.

"Did you get a blood test?" I asked, hoping the answer was no.

Green gave me another silly look. "We haven't talked in a while," he said.

Not only was Green an irresponsible jackass, he was now a father. I gave the only possible response for such a situation. "Wow," I said.

My mind raced. I was slowly getting pissed as I thought about how stupid Green was for getting himself in a baby situation on top of everything else. I knew all about his silly situation—how he'd fallen apart because his maybe baby momma didn't want him. She left him for a one-legged Mexican. The whole situation was beyond pathetic, and I was the one who had to pay for it.

I'ma bout to cuss Green the fuck out, I thought to myself. *I can't believe this shit. He's runnin' round happy he got some stupid bitch pregnant, laid up in my house. He's so concerned 'bout that girl, he didn't give a damn that he fucked me over. Fuck that.*

I turned to face the microphone.

Sensing what was coming, the judge said, "I'm gonna end this right now. You'll get your money." He looked at my case again and exhaled. "According to Michigan law, all you get is three thousand dollars." He turned and looked at Green. "Son, you got to do better. Case dismissed."

Lucy met me at the double doors. "You tried," she said.

She knew that I had taken a beating out there. It wasn't half as easy as she'd made it seem. No one had ever handled me like that. *Judge Joe Brown is the meanest person I've ever met,* I thought to myself.

I looked at her and gave a half smile. "I won my case. And I didn't have to fight for it," I said.

Lucy nodded in understanding. She smiled and walked away.

Myra approached me next. "Thank you," I said to her.

It would be the last time I would see or hear from Myra again. It almost felt like I was leaving a friend behind.

The sound technician came over to me. He gave me a hug. "I can't wait until your book comes out," he said. Excited, he unhooked the microphone. He looked at me again. His cocoa complexion gleamed with enthusiasm. "I can't wait until your book comes out," he said again.

Myra and I exchanged unsure glances. I smiled, not knowing what to say, so I said replied, "Thank you." I was beyond ecstatic. He was my first fan.

The sound technician, sensing that he was being a bit over the top, gave me another hug and left me alone with Myra. Myra and I went over the final details as to how I would receive my check. I kept my cool. Myra could likely tell that I was still rattled, but she never let on. Before I walked back down the stairs and out to the cab waiting for me, I gave Myra a hug. "Merry Christmas," I said to her.

She gave me a smile, and I left.

I did nothing for the rest of the day except walk around downtown. I left my room and headed up the street toward the large office buildings, hoping to find a good steak restaurant. I wished that I would see some stars. I dreamed that Britney Spears and her paparazzi would drive by. All I wanted was one glance.

A bus was approaching a stop a few blocks from my room. People waited at the bus stop. I thought about catching the bus to see where it would take me but decided against it. *Don't be stupid, Nova*, I told myself. *It's getting late. You don't know where that bus is gonna take you or how long before it gets back. Let the bus go. Stay in your area.*

I walked on. I didn't turn any corners on my journey, so that it would be a straight shot back to my room. While walking, I took out my camera, flipped it open, and began taking pictures.

"Are you making a movie?" A middle-aged, black man asked. He left the crowd at the bus stop and ran over to me.

"No, I'm not. Sorry. It's my first time in LA. I'm just taking pictures."

"Darn," he said, smiling.

"If I was, I would put you in the movie."

He waved good-bye and went back over to the crowd.

I found a beautiful steak house a few blocks down the street.

The place was fancy and expensively decorated. The waiter brought me lemonade to drink as I looked over the menu.

"Excuse me, I have a question," I said. "The price for the steaks—does that include side items, or is that just the price of the steak?" I asked.

The waiter looked at me. He was a skinny, young white man with sandy brown hair and a friendly face. "Sorry," he said. "All our items are à la carte. Yeah, I know, it's really expensive."

I looked at the menu. "Welcome to LA," I said, and the waiter and I laughed.

I told him that I wanted chicken alfredo, and he directed me to a place next door. "You'll like it there. And it's more reasonably priced," he told me.

We chatted as I finished my lemonade. He told me he was from Idaho and had been in LA a little over eight months. He liked his new life in LA. The tips were great, and he had found a good roommate. He was slowly coming up in life. The waiter was nice. He even let me have the lemonade for free. When I was done, I thanked him and headed next door.

I loved my dinner at the Italian restaurant. I ate my chicken alfredo in peace.

Three young Hispanic girls sat at the table across from me having a meeting. I noticed them because the girl facing me looked like a model. Even more impressive she was incredibly smart. She looked to be no more than sixteen, and she was already spearheading a project. She delegated orders to the other girls, who wrote her ideas down on a notepad.

I watched the childlike woman with increased interest. I thought about what my friends and I were doing at her age. By the time I was sixteen, most of my friends had babies. All we wanted out of life was a low-income apartment and a used car. I was glad to see young girls with a different state of mind.

The girl stopped talking when she noticed me staring. I looked away. I wanted to tell her that I was proud of her and her friends.

I paid for my dinner with the money the show had given me. I even left the waitress an extra large tip, considering that the meal was free.

I walked around the area close to my hotel room. Express clothing store took up nearly a whole city block. A multitude of stores filled the plaza where my hotel was located. I walked around checking out the stores. I ordered a fresh-squeezed orange juice from the smoothie store.

I went back to my room and made a few phone calls before I dozed off. I talked to Jonathan and Mom. Mom was happy that I had won. She hadn't talked to Green yet. Next I called Chip, a good friend of mine. "I won my case," I told him.

"Wow, Nova. I'm so happy for you. So how was it?"

"Awful. It was so stressful. Green, he went up there actin' like he was happy to be on TV. He didn't even say sorry. He was gettin' smart with the judge. He made a damn fool out of himself."

Chip and I talked about court a while longer before he said, "You know, Nova. We've been on the phone twenty minutes, and all you've talked about was your case. You haven't said nothin' 'bout Hollywood or TV. That's how I know you were for real."

I paused for a moment, thinking about his comment. "I didn't do it for fame, Chip. I did it for money. I couldn't care less about TV. Yeah, I was for real. Green trashed my condo and left me with a ten thousand dollar-bill. I had to sue him. There was no other way to get my money. I had to do the show."

I was upset that Chip or anyone would think that I had undergone such an extremely inconvenience situation just to get on TV. I wasn't fame hungry. It wasn't until I looked up into the eyes of a real-life celebrity that I realized what I'd done. Before that, I'd thought about Judge Joe Brown as any other judge, so I'd focused solely on proving my case.

I chatted with Chip a few minutes longer, and then I ended our conversation. I was exhausted, mentally and physically.

The next morning, I dressed, checked out of my room, and left for the airport.

I loved the treatment I received in LA.

Once again my plane had engine troubles and was delayed at the LAX airport. I sat in the waiting area people watching and sadly reflecting over what had happened to me and what was to come.

While I was waiting, a middle-aged white man came over and sat down in the adjoined seat behind me. He was handsome and expensively dressed. He stared at me. Clean shaven; dark brown hair with no hint of gray; soft, brown, serious eyes—he was definitely a businessman. He turned to face me. "So why are you in LA?" he asked.

"I sued my brother on Judge Joe Brown," I said, not shy about my experience.

Yet this time there was no excited gleam in my eye. I was devastated and couldn't stop thinking about all that I had just gone through.

"Are you an actress?" he asked.

"Yes," I said, joking.

He rolled his eyes and turned away, uninterested.

I wanted his attention back so I said, "Naw, I'm just kidding. I'm a writer. At least that's what I go to school for."

I gave him my school line twice more and then stopped. He wasn't interested anymore. All I had to talk about was college, and once I noticed I was rambling on, I silenced myself. I turned away from him and looked sadly at the people walking by.

"You're a writer huh?" the businessman asked me after a moment had passed.

"Yeah, I go to Western Michigan University," I said, proudly.

He looked me over, and I looked him over. He was dressed different than most men I knew—rich and sexy. He had on a blazer with a vest underneath and some kind of collar shirt underneath the vest. He didn't wear a tie. He was dressed like the rich white men from the East Coast, the Hugh Hefner type, and I liked talking to him.

He wanted to know why I'd sued my brother. I gave him the basic rundown of what had happened with the condo, Green and the association.

I looked at the man. He seemed interested, so I began telling him what Judge Joe Brown had had to say. "Judge Joe Brown used Green as the example of what's wrong with young black men today," I told him. "He was mad that Green had trashed my condo. Here I am, a young black girl in school trying to make it, and my brother comes along and tries to tear me down." And then my temper softened. "But the judge also had some interesting things to say to me to. I told the judge that, when I lived in the condo, the neighbors were hostile toward me. He was like, 'Yeah, because they took one look at your family and labeled you.'"

I shook my head, thinking. "They did label me," I said, hurt. He looked at me sadly. He remained quiet as I thought for a moment.

I nearly shuddered as I remembered the cynical look on the judge's face.

I'd been stunned. I'd had no response. I thought about the card parties and and realized that I had labeled myself. Suddenly, the truth dawned on me. I was nothing but a hood rat, or at least it seemed that way.

But it was still hard for me to believe that Green had turned my house into a crack house. Perhaps Green hadn't done that. There were no police reports. In fact, no one had ever called the police. A trashed condo didn't equal drug trafficking. There was no proof of the violations. I hadn't talked to any of the witnesses myself, and the association president had told me during our meeting that the association held private meetings where they'd discussed my property specifically.

*   *   *

"How many meetings have you had?" I asked the association president politely during my private meeting with the association board. We met back in late September. Green had been gone a few weeks yet I was still receiving violations. I decided that it was time to talk to the association face to face.

"About three or four," she said, her head held high.

"We know what's going on over there because we have the neighbor across the street watching the house. She calls us whenever something's happening," another member of the board chimed in.

I was beyond pissed. I couldn't believe what she was telling me. This group of women got together to sip coffee and plot— all about me and my condo. They even had round-the-clock surveillance.

*   *   *

I didn't tell the man how and why I'd been labeled. I didn't tell him about the card parties I'd thrown either. And I didn't tell him about the fight with the association. I didn't tell him because he was white and I didn't want to offend him and because I thought that, in some way, he would side with the association. Most people did.

He listened, and his look softened. "I used to own a rental property in New York," he told me. "I rented it out to low-income people." He paused momentarily. "Black people …"

I understood. I was looking for Section 8 renters before I found Keydah because they were guaranteed rental income. The government paid for them. And the truth was that most Section 8 people were African American.

I gave him a slight nod, and he continued. "And it would start off with no problem. The mother and the kids would be there, and there would be no problems. Then the father would come in. He always got in—whether it was through the door or the window."

He stopped talking and gave me a moment to think. I understood.

I nodded, and the businessman continued. "And he would trash the place and break everything up. It got to the point that we had to have an on-site manager to keep them out." He stared at me, patiently. "To get out of that type of mentality, it takes intense reprogramming and reconditioning."

I absorbed his meaning. I'd seen angry baby daddies destroy property many times. It had happened to Yellow. In Yellow's case her baby-daddy had picked an argument with her and during the argument went crazy and began breaking all her things. Climbing in through the window when no one was home was new to me—a New York game—but it was the same old thing.

"Here's what I was thinking," I explained. "I was thinking that Green, being my brother, would go out there and act like me. I thought that the worst he might do is stiff me on the rent and try to get over like that."

At that moment, I gave the man a long stare, and he returned my gaze with the same look in his eyes. He understood what I meant. I'd never expected for Green to be perfect. I'd known that, for the most part, Green would try and get a free ride in one way or another because, thought it's sad to say, that's how most black men are.

I continued, shaking my head sadly. "I never thought that he would get out there and act the way he acted. I never saw it coming. I'm in shock."

The businessman stared at me for a moment and said, "I have three kids, and they all have different personalities. You think that because you're family, you can inject yourself into someone, but you can't. People are all different."

I sat silent, rethinking his advice. I was not my brother, and even though we were family, we had separate paths. My hatred for Green subsided some. I realized that I could only control me.

While I talked to the man, he stared at me; his gaze was serious, intense, and penetrating. He stayed focus on me, keeping my attention as I explained about going off to college and leaving my home. Then I talked about the association bill. "I don't have ten thousand dollars," I cried.

Hearing my revelation, his look intensified. I got the feeling he wanted to tell me something but couldn't say it.

It was time to go. "I gotta catch my flight," I told him.

He looked sad. He didn't say good-bye. He kept his eyes on me as I stood and grabbed my coat and purse. He looked me up and down. He paused at my purse and shoes. I had no designer bag, no designer jacket. My shoes were cheap and old. For the first time, I felt somewhat ashamed of my financial status. But the look he gave me let me know it didn't matter. So I smiled at him and said good-bye.

He looked as if he wanted to keep in touch, or maybe he was savoring the last minutes of our life together. I absorbed him, his style, his essence, and that look. I looked back one last time after I gave the stewardess my ticket. He watched me with his legs folded casually in front of him. I noticed how tall he was. That was the last time I looked back.

I feel asleep on the way back to Chicago. We were in the air for eight hours, and at some point, I became tired of looking at rivers, mountains, and clouds. When I awoke, snow and gray skies were all around me.

We landed in Chicago. Back at Chicago O'Hare, I was once again irritated by the poor service and delayed flight. This time I was calm. By now I was used to it. Besides, more black people were out, and they looked at me as if I was crazy as I stormed about trying to find my newest terminal and get answers as to why my flight was being delayed. At some point, I realized that the best thing to do was relax, and I would get home eventually.

I found my terminal. Once I knew where I had to go, I felt comfortable. I went back to the pretzel stand that I had passed on the way. I made sure to remember the exact turns so I wouldn't get lost.

I sat down to eat my pretzel. While munching away, a white man sat down in the chair adjacent to mine. I turned to face him.

"Where are you going?" he asked me.

"I'm going to Lansing," I said. "I live in Kalamazoo right now though."

I figured that he would know Lansing, considering it was the capital of Michigan. I never imagined that he would have heard of Kalamazoo.

"Really?" he asked me surprised. "I live in Kalamazoo," he said.

"For real? Get outta here; that's crazy," I said, stunned.

We began chitchatting, and the conversation soon moved to LA. Since our trips had already taken place and we were both returning home—he just for the holidays—we talked about where we'd been.

"I'm coming from LA. I sued my brother on Judge Joe Brown," I said.

"You did?" he asked interested. "When will the show air?"

"Sometime in March they told me. It has to go through editing first."

He nodded his head. "So what do you do?"

"I go to Western. I'm taking up creative writing. I write books. I already wrote a book. It didn't get published. I needed an editor. So I went to school for creative writing; hopefully I can get my next book published."

He had a serious look and he watched me close, but he had a different aura than the last gentleman I'd spoken with at LAX. This man wasn't as aggressive, not as intense. Something was very different about him; he was peaceful, serene, and laid back. He was soft spirited.

I tried to talk only about positive things. I didn't tell him about my job at GM because that only depressed me. And when we got to why I sued Green on the Judge Joe Brown show, I tried to keep it as simple as possible. I didn't mention that I still hated Green or that, although Green had walked away free and clear, I still owed the association $10,000.

I told him what the man in LA had told me. I wanted to

know what he thought because, on the plane, I had a revelation about myself. I repeated to him the story of the rental property in New York.

"The man told me that getting out of that destructive, lower-class mentality requires intense reprogramming and reconditioning. I thought about it while I was on the plane. I thought about where I come from. That's what Western has been for me—intense reprogramming and reconditioning," I said, holding back tears.

My life at Western had evolved into more of a self-reflecting meltdown than a carefree college experience. I confessed that making the transition was hard. Constantly reminded of the person I was, it was difficult to merge into the person I wanted to be.

I was being held back, and I knew it. I thought about the woman on the plane. I was right. The reason I couldn't make it was because of my race—in part because I'd come from the lower class of my race. I was tired of being reprogrammed and reconditioned. I just wanted to be me, and that wasn't good enough.

The man didn't know my inner thoughts, and I didn't know his. He sat quietly thinking. Then he told me about his life and what he'd had to do to get to where he was.

"I've been living in China for the last two years," he said. "I work for a company overseas."

"Wow, that's amazing," I said, impressed.

He gave me a slight nod. "Before that, I used to own a bed and breakfast. My wife and I had already raised our kids, and we had a large house in the country. My wife wanted to open a bed an bath and put people in the extra bedrooms. That's what she wanted to do, so we did it," he said, casually, as if opening a nursing home was no big deal. "I had a good job in Kalamazoo. I was overseeing shipment at a company for Phizer. I quit my job so I could help my wife full time with the bed and breakfast. We struggled for the first two years, and then we started making money. We did that for a few years. Then I got offered my job in China. A position opened, and my company wanted me to go. It was a great opportunity. I wanted to do it. So we sold the bed and bath and moved to China."

Wow, I thought to myself. *Now I don't feel so bad about leaving my condo.*

"You said you're an English major, right?" he asked me.

"Yeah."

"You know you can do a lot with an English degree. They're always looking for people to teach English. You can make a lot of money going around the world teaching English. They need English teachers badly in China. You see, as the world becomes more Westernized, people need to be taught English. Go to China. There you will learn a new culture."

I looked at him intently. "Can I ask you a question? Does your wife like China?"

He looked at me. I wanted the truth, and he knew it. He thought for a moment. "At first she had a difficult adjustment. As time went on, she got used to it and she liked it."

I nodded and gave him a smile. For the first time in my life, I gave leaving America serious thought.

"Last call for Lansing," I heard the flight attendant say.

"Oh no. I gotta go," I said to the man. "I almost missed my flight." I stood and looked at him. "Perhaps I'll see you in Kalamazoo." His eyes lit up for a moment as I gave him a slight smile.

He looked disappointed as I hurried away. So was I. I wanted to continue our conversation.

My mind was filled with thoughts of China as I hurried over to the attendant. "You almost missed your flight," she said, irritated.

She was a young, black woman. I didn't hear the announcement," I said.

"We've called your flight twice already. You were busy talking."

We exchanged looks as I handed her my ticket. I turned and looked back at the man still sitting, watching. I waved good-bye. He didn't wave back. He sat and watched me disappear down the stairwell and out to the waiting shuttle-bus that would take me up to the small jet.

I would remember those conversations when things became too difficult. And my life would become more difficult. When the show aired, the condo situation took on a new life. It was one thing for people to hear about drama. They said a quick word or two and then moved on to the next topic. But to see it on television made people feel as if it was their drama too.

Watching me on TV brought people into my world. They felt as if they had a right to comment. After all, they'd seen my drama on Judge Joe Brown. And that was difficult—on top of the stress of figuring out how to deal with the association, now I had to deal with public opinion.

CHAPTER FIFTEEN:
Air Time

JONATHAN AND I SPENT the holidays together – just the two of us, for the most part. I cooked my own holiday dinner. Thanksgiving was practice to see if I could pull off Christmas dinner. On Thanksgiving, I decorated the table with a beautiful fall-themed tablecloth. I didn't make a turkey, but I bought a large turkey breast, sliced it, and served it on a serving platter decorated with mint leaves and raspberries. After I ate, I called my family in Lansing and wished them all a happy thanksgiving.

On Christmas, I did the same. I set up our Christmas tree in the living room in front of the large picture window. I found a nice, solid red table cloth at the dollar store and went with that. I even invested in new holiday dishes.

I took my time setting everything up. Chip, a friend I'd met a few months earlier, stopped by for dinner. He walked in my apartment and looked around. I could tell that he was impressed by my arrangement. He even told me so.

I'd told Chip about Green and the condo situation. Chip was smart; he had great wisdom and advice for me. He said, "The Bible talks about that. It says that a man's greatest enemy is in his home. That ain't yo' friends pimp; that's yo' family. You can't get mad at them because that's the type of people they are. Your brother would do the same thing to me if given the chance."

I looked over at him. "You're right," I said. "If you left five hundred dollars lying around and Green was there, he would steal it without a second thought. I would tell anyone to hide their money when Green's around. I wouldn't leave a penny in his sight."

Chip laughed, and we continued talking. I liked Chip right away. Chip had a dark past. He had served eleven years in prison for narcotics distribution. He was even one of the main drug dealers in prison. I loved hearing his prison stories because, of all the men I'd met who'd come out of prison, Chip told the most interesting stories.

That Christmas, we ate a great dinner. I made the turkey the same way I had for Thanksgiving, except I used cranberries instead of raspberries. I made baked macaroni and cheese, candied yams, corn on the cob, rice and gravy, and baked spaghetti. I made a box cake and bought a sweet potato pie. My only flaw was that I burned the corn bread. Other than that, it was a perfect dinner.

I was happy that, for the first time ever, I awoke with presents under the tree. And I wasn't at Grandma's house. I was home. I showed Chip my new coffee maker and foot massager.

"I bought her that," Jonathan said proudly.

"He did," I said, handing Chip the box my foot massager had come in. "I wanted to start a gift exchange with Jonathan this year. I didn't know how to start our tradition. I knew I didn't want to be with Jonathan when he purchased his gift for me. That way, it would be a complete surprise. I wasn't sure what to do. I asked my friend about it, and he said, 'Take Jonathan to Target to do his shopping. You don't have to be with him while he's there. Give him to one of the people workin'. They'll walk with him while he shops.' I was like, 'For real? I won't be botherin' nobody?' He was like, 'Naw, you good. The people at Target are cool. I work for Target. If someone came in and wanted me to walk with her kid so her kid could do some holiday shopping, I would.' So I did just that. The helper at Target was nice. She seemed happy to take Jonathan around. Afterward, I took Jonathan home, and he wrapped my gifts in his room. I woke up this morning so happy. Do you know that this is the first Christmas ever that I woke up with presents under the tree for me?"

"Wow, Nova. That's so different," Chip said. We sat on the large, chocolate sofa watching TV. He looked over at me, smiling. "I'm so happy for you. Despite all of that, you still figured out a way to make a good Christmas for you and your son. You know this is my first Christmas. I came in and saw all the decorations on the table and how everything was set out and was so impressed."

"Awe," I said. I gave him a warm smile as I placed my head on his shoulder.

I couldn't understand why he had never had a Christmas. It seemed that before and after prison he would have had a Christmas. I didn't press the issue. It was our first Christmas together, and I was happy about that.

"This is the best Christmas I've ever had," I told Chip. "For the first time, there's no drama on Christmas. Last year, all we did was fight. Even when company came, we still fought."

Whether or not the family wanted me home for Christmas didn't matter. Even though a year had passed, I was still traumatized from the Christmas before. This year, 2007, had turned out to be my craziest year on this planet. Despite the ups and downs, I wanted to end the year with peace.

I brought in 2008 alone in the house with Jonathan. I slept on the couch until Jonathan woke me up just a minute before the ball dropped on CNN. "Come on, Mom, the ball's 'bout to drop," he said, shaking me awake.

I hopped up off the couch and rushed into the kitchen. I grabbed the bottle of alcohol-free wine I had bought just for the occasion. I poured the drink into two wine glasses and handed one to Jonathan.

Jonathan and I did the ten second countdown together. "Happy New Year," we sang out as the papier-mâché' blanketed New York.

Out of all the New Year's I'd enjoyed—drinking at the club, traveling to different cities, partying with friends—being at home toasting with my son was the best New Year I'd ever had.

That February, I turned in my CTS. I spent hours on the internet looking at cars. I had my money from Judge Joe Brown plus my financial aid refund check. Now that I was a junior in college, I received enough in government aid to pay my entire tuition and fees.

In total, I had $5,000. I decided to spend the money on a large down payment for a new car. I had dented credit, and I was worried about my options. I knew that I needed a low car note and a late-model car. I also wanted good gas mileage because gassing my Cadillac kept me broke.

I found my 2005, red and chrome Chevy Cobalt LS at Deenoyer Chevrolet. After I got the car rust proofed and bought tire blowout protection, my payments were $175 a month, a savings of $161 monthly. (My Cadillac payments had been a little over $336 per month.)

My auto insurance went from $240 a month to $145 a month. In the end, I saved myself $256 a month just by turning in my car. I was beyond thankful. I knew I would need the money.

It hurt not having my Cadillac. No longer did people stare at me in traffic. I was a regular person again, at least I felt regular—that is, until the showed aired.

A postcard arrived in the mail one day postmarked from the Judge Joe Brown show—the show would air on Monday, March 16, 2008. I let everyone know. I had recorded TV at the time, so I programmed my television to record the show.

Jonathan and I had seen the commercial on television that Friday. I was ecstatic when I saw myself on TV. My skin looked smooth and clear, my ponytail was shiny, and my makeup was flawless.

Once I saw that I looked good on TV, I was relieved.

Jonathan laughed hard when he saw the commercial premier. On the commercial, they showed the part where I asked Green if he had a son. Then they cut to the clip of him recoiling and saying, "Whoa." All I could do was laugh. They made it seem like a Maury situation.

I watched the show for the first time with Vernon, who I'd been in touch with on and off since he helped me shop for my television appearance outfit, and Jonathan. (I wished I could have watched the show with Chip, but he'd disappeared from my life shortly after Christmas).

Vernon picked me up from school the day the showed aired. I was in class during its first run. I was glad I had recorded TV. I was taking a poetry class that semester. I liked the class, and we shared things about ourselves. I told them about the show. They wanted me to bring in a tape, but the show didn't sell individual tapes.

Vernon and I talked briefly about the show on the short trip to my house. Mondays and Wednesdays were my late days, so Jonathan would already be home when I got there.

I walked down the dark, musty staircase; hurried to apartment 13; and unlocked the door.

Jonathan turned around. "Hey, Mom," he said.

"Hey, Jonathan. Come on, let's watch the show."

The three of us sat in the living room silently as the show came on.

"Look at you," Vernon said. I glanced over at him and gave him a slight smile. All I could do was shake my head in silence.

I studied myself. On camera, I looked calm yet very sad. I could see the sadness on my face and the pain in my eyes. I could hear the hurt in my voice. I began to feel depressed as I watched myself.

Then the view changed, and I got to see Green. At first Green seemed cocky. It looked as if he had it all together, but as I listened, I got to see what a fool he made of himself.

Green was made to look like a fake drug dealer, and I was the innocent sister who he'd taken advantage of. The commentator had us laughing. She gave a brief overview of Green's actions after the commercial break. She told the viewers that Green was selling drugs and causing a disruption, "ruining his sister's good name," she said.

I laughed. "Yeah," I said. "Green ruined my good name."

The three of us chuckled, and I continued watching the show. It was over quickly. The editors had cut out my question about Green being a drug dealer because he was black. And they'd cut out my comment about being afraid of white men on the street. I was glad. I didn't want to seem racist on national television because I'm not a racist person. I acknowledge race and the impact it has on humanity, but I'm not a racist.

The second time I watched the tape was with my friend, Remy; her guy friend, Ramon; and two of his friends. We smoked a blunt, and I played the tape. The group tried to laugh and clown, but the show was no laughing matter. Soon, they found little to laugh about. They chuckled at Green's smart comments and how the judge shut him down at every turn, but there wasn't much else to say. They knew how I felt about the situation in real life. I didn't want to laugh.

"The show wasn't about you. It was more about your brother. He was the one clownin' tryin' ta get smart with the judge," Ramon said.

I nodded in agreement. The show wasn't about me. I never got my Jerry moment. For the most part, I remained calm and quiet. Green was the real asshole, so he stood out more. I didn't care about Ramon's comment. I wasn't trying to become a star; I simply wanted my money.

Deshaun, Ramon's friend, cut in. "I get it," he said. "Ya'll went out there, hood rat'n it up, and pissed those white folks off. And they came after you."

I looked over at him. "That's sounds about right," I said.

I let out an exhausted sigh. I had to take some of the blame, but for the most part, what had happened was Green's fault. Even though I had fun watching Green's demise on national television, I wasn't satisfied. I wanted more. I wanted real justice. And I wasn't the only one who felt that way.

Back in November, right before I did the show, I went to visit Remy. Ramon and a few of his friends were over. I began a casual conversation with one of the boys, and soon we began talking about my condo.

Remy looked over at me and gave me a knowing smile. All we did was get high, and once I was high, I went on a Green rant.

She knew what was coming, and so did I. As we passed the blunt back and forth, chatting about no-good people in the street, my mind immediately fell upon Green. Green was worse than the strangers in the hood. He was worse than the white folks. He was my brother.

"Yeah, I rented my condo out to my brother and two of his friends," I began telling the guy I'd struck up a conversation with. "They trashed my condo and left me with a ten thousand dollar-bill."

The boy looked amazed. "What! Huh? How the fuck did that happen? I'ma tell you how that happened. Your brother bitched up and didn't handle them niggas. I'll tell you what, let some of my friends fuck up my sister's condo, and see what I do. I'ma be fuckin' niggas up left and right."

The boy began bouncing in his seat. He appeared angry as he thought about it. Remy and I smiled, and I began laughing. I was glad that he cared. It was a terrible thing that Green had done.

"You're right," I told him. "That's the same way I felt. I felt like Green shoulda did somethin' to those boys for fuckin' up my house. He didn't do shit to them. I bet you they still friends."

I'd thought about having a friend or two pay Green a visit to give him a nice working over and make him wish he would not have trashed my condo .I had a good friend of mine who would have done me the favor for free.

"If I woulda' had a husband, this would have never happened to me," I told my friend, Jonah. "My husband woulda slapped the fuck outta Green for fuckin' up my condo."

"If you were my wife, I woulda beat Green's ass for you. I can still do it if you want me to," Jonah said.

"You'd beat up Green for me?" I asked, not able to hide the newfound love I felt for him.

Jonah thought it over a moment or two. He knew Green personally, and there could have been serious problems if he would have done the deed personally.

"No," he said. "But I can have a couple of my homeboys from

Flint come down and fuck him up. They'll come down, fuck Green up, turn around, and go back to Flint. Just like that. It ain't nothin'."

I thought it out a moment or two. *No, Nova, Mom will kill you if you had somethin' happen to Green. You'll just end up in prison. Besides, that's your brother.*

"No, Jonah, that okay," I reluctantly responded. "I'm not gonna do nothin' to Green. I'll just end up bringing more drama to my life."

"Uh-huh, well let me know if you change your mind."

"I will."

I never changed my mind. I stuck to my word that I wouldn't directly cause Green harm. But I remained adamant in my gestures of recluse against Green and I continued to avoid him. And I was justified in doing so.

I watched Green on TV, degrading my home, my life, and my well-being while he mentioned nothing of his friends or their responsibility. Green took the fall, and he was blaming me for it. I had no respect for him. I was constantly disgusted.

I watched the show for the third time with Raheem. He started off sitting next to me, but as he watched the show, he came over and laid his head across my lap. Raheem remained silent as he rubbed my leg and paid attention.

Raheem and I had talked about the situation on a regular basis. He knew the story from the beginning. To watch it on TV saddened him the same way it saddened me. After the show, I fired up a blunt and silently smoked. Raheem quietly looked on.

I learned the most when I stopped paying attention to how I looked on TV and listened to some of the answers Green gave. "Do you love your sister?" I heard Judge Joe Brown ask Green.

Green looked at the judge with evil in his eyes and said, "To death."

I missed that part in court, but I heard it the sixth time I watched the show. For fun one day, Jonathan and I watched the show again. Hearing those words on TV made me look at my relationship with Green different.

In April, I began pushing the show to the back of my mind. I had more important things to worry about than Green and Judge Joe Brown. First and foremost, I focused on school. I studied day and night. Jonathan and I were at the library most nights of the week. He played on the computer while I wrote my papers and studied for my exams. Even on the weekends I was devoted to schoolwork. I figured that graduating was the only way to change my life.

On Friday, April 27, the spring semester ended. That Wednesday after grades came out, I sat at my dining room table. In front of me, I had my checklist for graduation. I watched Jonathan play his video games as I entered in my grades.

After every semester, I went over my checklist. I tallied up all my credits and smiled. I was officially a senior. I counted and recounted my credits to make sure, and it was true. My calculations were correct. I had 103 credits. (I only needed 88 to be a senior.)

Unlike during my seven years at LCC, at Western, I was focused and dedicated. It had taken me a long time to earn my associate's degree. It had been an exhausting journey, and I'd learned a lot on the way. Yet nothing could prepare me for Western. My time at Western was quick.

At WMU I was brought up to speed. Western did for me what LCC couldn't. Western got me over my high school experience. I no longer thought about my days at J. W. Sexton High. College erased all that.

I can't believe this shit. My dumb ass is about to graduate from college, I thought, as I penned in the last grade. I read over the English department checklist. Only two major classes and two semesters of foreign language, and I would be done with school.

I compared all my lists—my major requirements, my minor requirements, and WMU's required courses. The required classes I still needed to graduate and the number of credits I needed for graduation coincided—an exact match.

After finishing all of the required classes for graduation, I would have 121 credits. I needed 122 to walk. To get that extra credit, I figured that I would take an independent studies course in the fall.

I relaxed in my chair. I turned to Jonathan and said, "We're outta here after graduation."

"Really?" He looked over at me surprised.

"Yeah. I'm almost ready to graduate. After the show aired, I decided that I wasn't going back to Lansing. I'm tired of fighting with the family."

"Where are we gonna go?"

"Don't know. I was thinking about the suburb of Detroit."

Jonathan looked worried. I figured I would give him some time. He would get used to the idea of moving to Detroit.

I turned back to my lists. I grabbed a blank piece of paper and made one long list. I wrote out all the classes I would take during my last three semesters at Western so I could visualize the end:

Summer I, 2008:
American Sign Language I
Summer II, 2008:
American Sign Language II
English/Practical Writing
Fall 2008:
History: African Civilization
Math 1140
Philosophy 1001
English: Advanced Creative Writing
Independent Study

That was it. Eight more classes, and I was done.

I sent Jonathan to Lansing to be with Mom as soon as school ended for him in mid-June. Since he would be living with Mom for most of summer semester, I would have time to concentrate on school and my fight with the condo association.

Chapter Sixteen:
Battle Cats

IN MAY, I STARTED my battle with the association. I decided to step things up. I felt as if the fight with the association was dragging on. I was still receiving excessive violation notices. They cited my new tenant for everything. The last notices I received complained about her children riding their bikes on the sidewalk. I didn't want to make Keydah pay $100 every time her children went outside to play. It was then that I knew that I had to do something drastic.

First, I needed a new attorney. I'd already fired Jenny several months earlier. She had made no progress with the association. I was tired of her runaround. She had no plausible solution to my problem.

When I called around to find another lawyer, I realized why Jenny hadn't been more helpful.

"My retainer is ten thousand dollars for a case like this," the third lawyer told me. "Honestly, you could easily spend more than ten thousand trying to fight them."

I thanked him for his time and continued calling around. Every attorney told me the same thing. They wanted more for their fee than the association was charging me.

I found a lawyer who would listen to me for free. He had an office in Okemos, Michigan, twenty minutes from downtown Lansing. I knew he had money because he was in Okemos; only people with money lived or had businesses in Okemos.

"How much do you charge for a case like this?" I asked him over the phone.

"Just come in and talk to me. I won't charge you anything for that."

I went to see Mr. Redding on May 17. He had a large office a few building from Dr. Washington. Mr. Redding's blue eyes were sharp and attentive as he listened.

After I finished talking, he leaned back in his chair and gave me a wicked smile. "Normally, I handle cases like this from the other side," he said. "I'm a corporate lawyer. Usually I spend my time knocking down people's discrimination cases." He let out a soft chuckle. "When a company has a problem like this, they call me." He looked at me, serious and firm. "I believe you have a case. In all the cases I've heard, yours is the most believable. I believe that you are being discriminated against." He thought for a moment. "I've had other clients who've had problem with associations. I had one client whose association was violating them all the time because they put up a swing set in the backyard. In the end, my clients got together with other neighbors who had swing sets and got them to throw out the people on the board and get a new board. Condo associations are just like high school. Everyone sits around in their groups picking on people."

You've given me a fabulous idea, I thought to myself as he talked. *When I get back to Lansing, I'm gonna get on the board. I'm gonna get those bitches out of there.*

It turned out that Mr. Redding was familiar with Brian Quaint and his law firm. "I've had to deal with them before," Mr. Redding told me. "They charge their clients a ridiculous amount. I was handling a corporate bankruptcy. Their client was suing my client for a million dollars. We offered to settle with them for one hundred thousand dollars, but they said no. In the end, all they got was a hundred and fifty thousand. But they paid two hundred grand in legal fees." He shook his head, seemingly pleased about the outcome. "They should have taken the settlement."

Mr. Redding looked at me. "You said you've got a tape?"

"Yes. I recorded my last meeting with the association back in March. I thought about the drug allegations a lot more. They told me that cars would pull up, wait twenty minutes, and come out.

That doesn't prove that my tenants were selling drugs out of the house. That could have happened only a few times."

Mr. Redding nodded in agreement. "Anything can be made to look like drug trafficking."

"Exactly. So the next time I met with the board, I brought it up again. They denied the drug charges once I started questioning them about it. They told me that they never said that my brother was a gang member or that they were afraid of gang retaliation."

I pulled a small tape from my briefcase. Mr. Redding got out his tape recorder and put the tape in. Silent, we listened to the tape.

Once I saw that the association was not letting up, I started playing hardball. The association was flabbergasted when I pulled out my tape recorder during our second meeting back in March.

"I hope you ladies won't mind me recording this conversation," I said to the board as I presented the tape recorder.

The woman with the dog story shook her head, frantic. Her curly perm bounced from side to side as she looked at the association members. "Can she do that? She can't do that," she said.

The president placed her hand on the woman's arm, calming her down. "Let her do it. We have nothing to hide."

I gave the woman a sinister smile as she closed her mouth. I hit the record button and we started our meeting.

I went back over what we'd discussed during out first meeting in November. "You said that there was drug activity going on in my house and you were afraid of gang retaliation," I said to the board.

The board members began shaking their heads, but no one spoke up. Before the board could think of a response, the woman with the dog story jumped in. "We never said that," she said.

The president and the rest of the board members, including the representative, looked stunned. They were going to try and talk their way out of the drug allegations, but the woman with the dog story was so determined to get me that she outright lied. Once she told me that lie, I knew everything else was a lie.

I was pissed. I called her out. "Yes, you did. In fact, you had the most to say. You told me a story about you walking your dog." I gave her an evil glare. "I should have recorded the first conversation too."

Mr. Redding listened to the tape a few minutes. Then he stopped the tape. "I'm going to listen to the rest later," he said.

Mr. Redding agreed to help me. He told me that he would write the association a letter. I gave him my file with all the information I had. Then I left for Kalamazoo.

Two weeks later, I met with Mr. Redding again. He had completed his letter. He had me come in and pick up my file. During our second meeting, I told Mr. Redding about my plans to fight the board directly. I also told him that I wanted to start a protest and boycott the association meetings.

With his sparkling blue eyes, Mr. Redding looked me over. I had on an old pair of yoga pants, a faded T-shirt, and a head scarf. I hadn't felt like getting dressed up that day. I stared back at him, taking notice of his straight, blond hair and neatly trimmed mustache. He leaned back in his chair. "You seem like the type," he said.

I sued my brother on Judge Joe Brown. I am the type. They keep fuckin' with me, and I'ma have Jessie Jackson up here, I thought to myself.

After talking to me a few more times, Mr. Redding told me the truth. "Let me be honest with you—and I thought this from the first time I saw you,"—he said. "You can't afford me."

I was silent because he was right. I could barely afford rent, let alone a corporate attorney. I wanted to cry because I knew what he was saying. He was letting me go. But before he did, he gave me some help.

Mr. Redding gathered up all the addresses of the people who had liens on their condos in Fairfield. Then he began filing a complaint for me with the Michigan Department of Civil Rights.

He explained to me how to finish the complaint and what I needed to say.

I thanked him for all his help. I knew Mr. Redding helped me to make up for all the people he'd screwed over fighting for corporations. I didn't have a dollar, and he probably figured I'd never pay him the rest of his fee. He charged me ninety-five dollars for the letter. And that's why I respected Mr. Redding, even after knowing the type of person he was. He was a man with a heart and a job to do.

"I want to help you," Mr. Redding told me during our first meeting.

I looked at him. It was the way the he said it that let me know he was sincere. He said it as if helping me redeemed him somehow. Mr. Redding was a genuine person because he did help me. I don't know how much time he spent on me, but it was more than I could afford. And it was the right help.

Mr. Redding schooled me on many things. "What about going to the media?" I had asked him over a telephone conversation.

"You don't want to do that just yet. Sometimes the media can get involved and mess things up. They can take sides, and the public gets involved. The Michigan Department of Civil Rights will do a fair investigation. And they'll handle things quietly. With the media, things can get out of hand."

I understood exactly what he meant. I decided that, whatever steps I took, I would play it smart.

Other people encouraged me to go to the media. Asia had landed a job as a news anchor back in March. In June, we talked about my case. She told me step by step how to get an investigation started. "Contact the investigation department at FOX 47 in Lansing. They'll talk to people and do all the investigating for you," Asia informed me.

I turned her down, telling her about Mr. Redding's advice. I wanted to be discrete around town.

I met with the association again in late May. This time, I brought Keydah with me. Keydah met me at the clubhouse. Since

Keydah lived within walking distance, she arrived first. I came just as the meeting was about to end. Another black woman was there addressing her concerns with the association.

The black woman was old and seemed as if she didn't want to fight. "I was just wondering why you keep giving me citations for having curtains up when I walk around the complex and seen six other people with curtains in their windows," she told the board.

"You have, which condo was it?" the president asked.

The black woman went on to explain which condo she lived in. The more I listened to her story, the more it didn't sound right.

"Well why are you giving her citations when there's other people with curtains up?" I asked on behalf of the black woman. "How long have the other people had their curtains up? You said that you sent the one man a notice months ago, but he hasn't taken his curtains down yet. Have you been giving him violations? How long are you gonna let him keep his curtains up before you start citing him like you have with this woman here?"

The board members glared at me. The black woman looked annoyed, as if I was butting into her business, so I let it go. Her story bothered me, but I didn't have time to investigate. I was there to fight my own battle.

Once the black woman left, I pulled out my recorder. Once again, the woman with the dog story was pissed. This time, she remained quiet though.

I got to the main reason I was there. I wanted Keydah to be able to live in peace. I wanted the citations against her to stop.

"So her children can't ride their bikes on the sidewalk ever?" I asked the board members.

"No, it's in the bylaws," the president said.

I was upset, and I let her know it with the look I gave her. "But other children ride their bikes on the sidewalk."

"We're not talking about everyone else."

"How do you know that it's her children riding their bikes? It could be anyone's children."

"We know that the children are hers," the president said.

"You know her children?" I asked.

"Yes, we do," she said, with a stern look on her face.

"How do you know my children?" Keydah asked. "What do you do—spy on me?"

I turned to Keydah. "They do spy on you. I know they do. They've told me. They take pictures of your house. They watch you. They know when you leave and when you come back home. I've read the e-mails. They watch you day and night."

Fairfield had begun releasing all the e-mails between the board members pertaining to my condo. Someone was sitting and watching my house and then e-mailing the association.

I'd read a few of the e-mails. They read like a story: "A man just pulled up blaring loud music. He parked in an assigned parking spot," the e-mail read. "Now the man just left again blasting his music," the second e-mail said. "Guess he still hasn't figured it out because he's back again parking in the assigned parking spot," the third e-mail read.

I was infuriated. I figured the woman across the street was the one doing the reporting. I had no idea who the man she'd seen was or if her story was even true. But I did know that every time an e-mail was sent, I was charged $100. The board never took my side. They always voted against me.

Keydah was pissed. The women on the board had no response. They looked at her silently. Angry, the board members told me to leave the meeting and never come back. I refused.

"I'm going to call Todd," the president said after I refused to leave.

The fact that she had threatened me with a white man sent me into a rage. "Go get Todd," I told her. "I don't care. Who is Todd? I have a right to be here just like you do. I own my home just like you. You have one vote, and I have one vote. I'm not gonna take this from you people." I stood up. "You've made a big mistake coming after me. You're gonna pay for this."

I grabbed my purse and headed toward the door with Keydah.

I flashed the board members a malicious grin before heading out. "You ladies have a nice day," I said, as I made my exit, glad to leave before they called the police.

"You too," the president said as she glared at me.

In the parking lot, Keydah and I talked. "I'm sorry I brought you into this. I can't believe that they won't let your children play on the sidewalk," I told her.

"It's no problem. The black woman in there was saying the same thing. She was like, 'I think you all are singling me out. I feel like I'm the only one being violated.'"

"Damn I wish I woulda got here a few minutes earlier. I woulda been all over them." I looked off into the distance as I thought. "This isn't fair. I don't know how I'm gonna make them pay, but I'm gonna get them back for this."

I left the meeting with a renewed determination.

The letter Mr. Redding wrote only pissed the association off more. They sent me a letter in June stating that, if I didn't pay the full amount, which was now over $12,000, I would be sued.

I talked to Topaz about the condo association as soon as I got the letter. "I can't believe this shit," I said. "It won't stop. Damn near every week, there's a new citation. I can't get any peace. All those bitches do is spy on me and write up citations. Now they're talking about suing me. I can't afford an attorney. My last attorney just let me go."

"I don't know what to tell you, Nova," Topaz said sadly. "Here, talk to my mom."

Topaz's mom gave me great advice. "You need to start a grassroots campaign. Contact every grassroots organization you can. You need outside help."

"I've filed a case with the Michigan Department of Civil Rights."

"That's a good start, but you need to contact them all."

It was then that I knew exactly what to do. I'd learned all about resistance from Africana studies. One class in particular, The History of Race and Class, taught me, step by step, how black people had fought white people and won. White people didn't get everyone, only those who didn't fight back. With all my knowledge and advice, I was ready.

The next day, I wrote a universal letter and addressed one to each specific organization I was sending it to. I'd found the names, numbers, and addresses for a number of civil rights organizations by conducting a Google search. I sent out my letter:

Dear ————

I am writing this letter in regards to my property at 6321 Beechfield Drive. Currently, I am renting my condo while away at college. Since I've been gone, the condo association has charged me over ten thousand dollars for various violations and fees. The association has claimed that the charges are due to my first tenant, who was allegedly trafficking drugs out of my home. This is not true. I rented my condo to my brother. My brother was not and is not involved in any drug activity. Once confronted about the drug allegations, the board then denied ever making such allegations.

To resolve the matter, I removed my brother from my property and leased my condo to another tenant, who is also African American. The association has excessively given her violation citations as well. The association has even given me citations during a period that my condo sat empty of renters.

At this time, I believe that I am a victim of housing discrimination. I am asking for your assistance in stopping the citations, disputing the ten thousand dollars in fees and attorney fees I've incurred, and providing me with legal assistance.

I appreciate your concern regarding this matter. If you have any questions, please contact me at the address and telephone number listed above.

Sincerely,
Nova M. Wallace.

My letter caught the attention of several civil rights

organizations. I started getting responses right away. By early July, I'd spoken to civil rights organizations from Chicago to Washington DC. I'd even contacted the NAACP in Lansing. Everyone I talked to wanted to help.

The people in Washington DC helped me to relax. "You have to calm down," the woman on the phone told me. "I know it's hard because it's happening to you, but these things take time. Just go on living your life, and let us take care of it."

A few days later, I spoke to another woman in Chicago who was outraged when I told her what was happening. She called me as soon as she got my letter. "That is just ridicules," she said, when I told her about Keydah's children not being allowed to ride their bikes on the sidewalk.

"Yes it is," I said. "It's like I can't live my life. This whole situation has consumed me. I don't know what to do, and no one wants to listen to me. Everyone treats me like I'm crazy because I think that the white people are out to get me."

"You just stay strong. This situation will get resolved."

I was glad to have people on my side. I knew that the women I spoke with over the phone were African American because of their dialect. I felt that I had been saved. I knew they would get the association off my back.

During that time, all I did was get high and trash talk Green and the association. I felt as if the two of them had, in some way, worked together to try and destroy me. To sum it all up, it sometimes seemed like the white people were trying to take everything I had, and a black man had handed me over to them.

Several organizations agreed to help me. With the different organizations aware of my problem, I was actually able to relax while I lived my life.

The Michigan Department of Civil Rights picked up my case. This organization handled it because of the type of case it was and the fact that I lived in Michigan. The organization I talked to in DC handled corporate cases.

The organization I talked to in Chicago offered to help. "We don't have as much power as the Michigan Department of Civil Rights. They can do everything you need. They can get the citations overturned and get you an attorney," the woman in Chicago told me. "Keep on trying with them. If they don't help, then we'll get involved. At the very least, we can write the association a letter."

The MDCR had branches in both Lansing and Kalamazoo. I talked to a Hispanic man at the Lansing branch. He told me to file my complaint in Kalamazoo because that was where I lived. So I did that.

I lost contact with the Chicago organization, but they didn't let me go so easily. The woman in Chicago called me and sent letters until the MDCR informed her that they were handling my case. She sent me a final letter letting me know that she had closed my case and that I could contact her if needed. She made me feel as if I had a friend because she cared about what happened to me just as much as I did.

The MDCR told me about their plan. The organization would start by sending a letter to Fairfield inquiring about the violation citations. Then they would start calling residents of Fairfield. If needed, the MDCR would do a door-to-door investigation.

The MDCR immediately started its investigation. They sent Fairfield a letter in mid-July. I stopped getting citations after that. For the first time in over a year, the mailman stopped knocking on my door to hand me certified letters from Fairfield. For the first time in a year, I was able to have peace at night.

I was glad I had professional help. In June, I tried to get my family to help me fight the association. I asked them to start going out to Fairfield and taking pictures of cars backed into spots, children playing on the sidewalk, and people committing other "violations" the association had cited me and my tenants with.

Earnest went out one day for me, but he gave up. "Nobody was doing anything. There were a couple of white girls riding their bikes, but I didn't want to start taking pictures of them. How would that look—me sitting around taking pictures of kids?"

You would look just like them when they sit out there taking pictures of my condo, I thought to myself.

I didn't get mad that he didn't want to help. I'd known he wouldn't. "That's okay. You tried. Thanks," I said. I never bothered him with it again.

Keydah had offered to help. She even sent me a picture of an unknown car parked in her parking space. I was glad for the help but felt that it wasn't enough. In reality, it could have been anyone's car. I didn't feel as if it would hold up in court.

The MDCR completed its investigation in early August. The result of the investigation was that I was one of many residents facing excessive violation fees from the association. I was not being singled out because of my race. The association's actions were not racially motivated.

The MDCR found several condo owners who'd had multiple liens placed on their homes by Fairfield. "I talked to a white woman," the MDCR investigator told me. "She had the worst story out of everyone. She said that the association stood outside her house for thirty minutes looking around and trying to find a reason to cite her. They finally found something and did so. I'm sorry. I don't think you're the victim of discrimination. The association is running a scam. They're doing this to get money out of the residents," she said, sad and disappointed that she couldn't help me.

I was silent a moment. "Thank you," I said. "At least now I know. I feel better knowing that they wasn't doing this to me because I'm black."

"Yeah, at least you don't have to live with that over your head. It does bring a peace of mind. I'm glad we could help."

I hung up the phone. I wanted to call her back. I had more to say. There was a part of me that was skeptical because the woman who headed the investigation was white. Then I thought some more. I had met with the investigator personally. Even though she was white, I felt that she was genuinely concerned about my case. She wanted to help me. I accepted the organization's decision.

I was thankful for the investigation. During this time, I had stopped trusting all white people. I began to think that they were all connected. I did gain peace of mind. Even though losing the investigation meant that I had disproved my only defense.

The association made its move, as I'd known it would. I found out that they had sued me back in late July. I received the notice of default in the mail sometime around the beginning of September. I called the court immediately. They told me to come down and file an appeal. I rushed down to Lansing the next day and filed my appeal. I got a court date.

I was beyond nervous about my court date. I was scared. I began crying whenever I talked about it or whenever I thought about it. I tried to stay positive, but it was hard. I knew what was coming—a loss. I had no real defense. I had no lawyer. I had no witnesses on my side. I had no case.

"Are you gonna put Green on the stand?" Topaz had asked me.

"No. After Judge Joe Brown, I don't trust Green. He's actin' like he wanna help, but he might get on the stand and totally fuck me over. After he stole Jonathan's Nintendo DS, I was done."

* * *

I'd picked Jonathan up from my mom's in mid-July. I let my nephew come and stay with us for the rest of the summer. Once we were back in Kalamazoo, the boys told me what had happened.

"Green stole Jonathan's DS, and he told me that he was gonna push you over the balcony if you tried to do anything about it," Donny told me.

I'd known that Green had something to do with the disappearance of Jonathan's DS when Jonathan told me about it as soon as the game system came up missing. Jonathan had fallen asleep with his DS by his side. According to Green, his son had gotten a hold of the DS and Green had taken it from him so that it wouldn't get lost. However, Green couldn't remember where the DS was, and so it was deemed permanently lost. Green agreed to pay for a new DS, but he never gave me all the money.

"But it's your fifty dollars," Green said to me after I told him I didn't want the rest of the money.

"No, Green, it's your fifty dollars. Besides, you already trashed my condo and left me with a ten-thousand-dollar-bill. What's fifty more dollars?"

I wasn't going to fight over small increments of money. It was late August. Green had been out of my life a year. I wanted nothing to do with him. I didn't want the DS money to keep us connected, so I let him keep it.

Besides, after Jonathan and Donny told me about the abuse they had to endure from Green, I felt it was best to leave Green alone. I'd already told Green that if he put his hands on my son again, I would call child protective services on him. I felt that Green was torturing my son because he couldn't get back at me. That was something I wouldn't tolerate. After my last threat, Green and I had an understood agreement to stay away from each other.

*   *   *

For the rest of September, I tried not to think about court. Before I knew it October 8 had come. I was glad to face the association in court. I was hoping that the board members would be there. But they weren't. They stayed sleep, safe in their beds, while I had to lug my sleeping child to Lansing at five thirty in the morning.

Court was scheduled for 8:30 a.m. on Wednesday, October 8. I brought Jonathan to court with me because it was too early for me to drop him off at school. I had to be on the road by 6:00 a.m., which meant I had to get up by at least 4:30 if I wanted a good start. I told him to be quiet and not say a word while we were in court. He nodded in understanding.

In the end, I had to appear in court to deal with the association's case three times. The first time, the judge delayed her ruling until the processor came in and testified that he had served me. I was adamant in my claim that I hadn't been served because I hadn't. So the judge rescheduled court for that Tuesday.

The judge wanted me to come back that Friday, but I couldn't. I had decided to move to Nashville instead of Detroit, and so I would be in Nashville that weekend looking for apartments. I was excited because my plan was to leave Kalamazoo on the day I graduated.

On the day of the second court date, an accident on the highway delayed me an hour. I ended up getting to court ten minutes late. I talked to the court secretary as soon as I got there. She told me to go downstairs and file another motion. The judge hadn't banned me from filing another motion, and so I still had a chance to see her.

I hurried downstairs and filed another appeal. I got a court date for the following Tuesday. That day, the judge was mad that I had missed the previous date. I tried to explain what had happened, but she wasn't listening. However, she did give me five minutes to drill the processor.

I was ready for the processor. I turned to the white man. He turned his body toward, me and we stared each other down. I was pissed that he was lying. He stuck to his story that he had served me the notice for court. I had never seen him in my life.

I never took my eyes off him, and he was up for the challenge. He stared back at me with the coldest blue eyes I'd ever seen. I quickly ran out of the four questions that I had written down. I had to go off the top of my head. I had to think quickly. I thought hard, using the full range of my knowledge, wisdom, education, and experience.

"You said that you approached the woman and asked if her name was Nova Wallace. At first the woman said yes, but when you handed her the notice, she changed her story and said no. Is that correct?"

"Yes," he said.

"And what did the woman do with the court papers?"

"She kept them."

She kept them. You lying bastard, I thought to myself.

I continued with my questioning. The look in my eyes was pure hatred as I stared the man down. He wasn't scared. He was ready. "You said that the woman was with two black men. Did you ask any of them to confirm the woman's identity?"

"No."

"And why not?"

"I didn't think I needed to."

"You didn't think you needed to. The woman disputed her identity. Why didn't you confirm who she was with the two men with her?"

"Uh, I don't know. You said that it was you."

The processor and I went back and forth, but he stuck to his story. I had known he would. He was probably paid for his testimony. It was then that I got to see exactly how innocent people were sent to prison. I was beyond pissed that the processor had claimed that I was with two black men when he served me. He just said that to make me seem easy.

When the judge ruled in the association's favor, I nearly screamed.

I turned and looked at Brian Quaint, who stood motionless and silent as he heard the news "I'm going to mobilize the black community," I said to him.

"Stop it. I'm not gonna let you use my courtroom to spread your rhetoric," the judge said.

I stared at the lawyer, ignoring the judge.

Brian never turned to look at me.

Then I thought about something better than the black community. "I'm going to the media," I said.

The attorney looked worried, but he remained cool.

I continued my rant. The judge threatened me. "I'm going to get an officer in here if you don't stop," she said.

I ignored her. The only thing that stopped me from slapping the processor in his face was Jonathan. I didn't want him to see me go to jail.

"If you want to go around telling everyone you meet about your case you can," the judge told me. "You're just not gonna do it in my courtroom."

I looked at her, pissed. "I'm not going to say anything. I'm going to write a letter."

I looked over at Brian. He seemed pale. Perhaps he remembered what happened to him the last time I wrote a letter and he had been investigated by the MDCR.

"I don't understand," I told the judge. "The violation fees started out around two thousand dollars. Now it's over sixteen thousand dollars. They've charged me four thousand dollars in interest since June. How can they do that?"

"I don't know," the judge said. "I'm not a lawyer. You should have gotten yourself an attorney."

"I can't afford an attorney. They took all my money."

"We gave you the number for legal aid," the judge said.

I rolled my eyes. "No one gave me the number to legal aid."

The judge turned to the court secretary and said, "Get her the number for legal aid."

Soon a bald-headed woman made her way over to me. Her dark skin seemed extra bright against the pale blue suit she wore. I wanted to snatch the number out her hands. She had sold me out, and she knew it. I didn't call her out on it; I gave her a break. Part of the problem was that the judge said it had taken me a day to file my last claim.

"I came here as soon as I got to Lansing. I talked to the woman …" I turned to point out the black woman, but she had quietly slipped out the courtroom. I turned back to the judge. "Conveniently, she's gone now. But I talked to the woman who was just sitting over there. She's the one who told me to go downstairs and file another appeal."

I took the card with legal aid's number and placed it in one of the folders inside my briefcase. The black woman never looked at me. She knew that she had helped them.

I can't believe they're doing this to me, I thought. *No one can stop them. They're all working together—one big circle of hands. This black woman knows she was in here last Tuesday. I talked to her. And she ain't gonna say shit.*

I left the courtroom still pissed. I followed behind the processor and the attorney from Fairfield. A woman walked behind me. Her job was to keep an eye on me. We stopped at the elevator. "Do you need me to ride down with you?" she asked me.

I turned to face her. "No, I'm gonna get another elevator. I want to ride with decent folks."

I let them go with no further words. I looked behind me. An officer had stepped silently into the hall. I knew that he was there to arrest me if I got out of hand. That angered me more than anything. I knew how white people worked. They were powerful creatures who banded together to get what they want. I had no one to help me, and I felt powerless to stop them.

I turned to Jonathan and gave him some words of wisdom. "I want you to remember this day," I said, loud enough for the officer to hear. "Never forget this day because this is what white people do to black people. They're thieves, and they steal your money. And when you try to protest, they take you to court. White people stick together, so they always win in court. And if you get mad and fight back, they lock you up. Look at me." I made Jonathan stare me in the eyes until I was satisfied that he understood the seriousness of our situation. "Never forget this. The white people stole your mother's money."

I made it back to my car. I called Asia and went off. "I can't believe this shit. I can't believe they just got me for sixteen thousand dollars. This is all Green's fault."

"Take the loss, Nova. Let it go, and take the loss."

"I don't wanna take the fuckin' loss. Green should be takin' the loss. This is all his fault."

"No, don't blame Green. Just let it go. Your association was some con artists; that's what it was."

Asia talked to me for almost thirty minutes. Eventually, the anger subsided and I went on with my life.

I spoke with legal aid soon after my last court appearance. They said that there was nothing they could to. They informed me that the association could not come after me because I was on Worker's Compensation, but once I started working again, they would. They told me to call them back once they come after me with the garnishment. They would try and help me get the payment down.

"Make sure you go to that court appearance," the receptionist told me. "If you don't, they can get the judge to award them any amount they want."

If they already lied about serving me once, why wouldn't they do it again? They probably will never tell me when the date is. They'll do the same thing. The processor will lie, and say he served me when he didn't. I won't be there in court, so they'll get whatever they want.

I didn't pass my complaint on to the woman on the other end of the line. I kept it to myself. I lost; that was it.

The final bill amounted to nearly $16,000. I spent over a year trying to rationalize what had happened. In the end, I took responsibility for my own actions and concluded that I shouldn't have given my nineteen-year-old brother the keys to my condo. That is the only thing that I could have done differently.

CHAPTER SEVENTEEN:
Graduation Day

I CHOOSE NASHVILLE AS my next city. I'd always loved Nashville. I'd visited Asia there and had a great time. Asia no longer lived in Nashville when I visited in October to find an apartment. She lived in Clarksville an hour away. She left Clarksville and met me in Nashville to help me find an apartment.

For three days, Asia, Jonathan, and I apartment hunted in Nashville. I found a beautiful apartment in Antioch, a suburb right outside Nashville. I loved my new apartment much more than I had the Whitehall apartments in Kalamazoo—no strange earwig bugs crawling around everywhere, no mold and mildew, and no tarnished fixtures in the kitchen and bathrooms. Beautiful landscaping replaced the bland exterior I was used to.

Even though I was going through a foreclosure, I was able to get my apartment. Once I got the acceptance call, everything was in place. Now all I had to do was make it through my last semester at Western.

I was taking five classes that semester, all difficult. I'd put off math to the very end. I hated math; it was hard for me. I had an English mind; I was creative. It was hard for me to grasp practical concepts. Philosophy was confusing. I took an African civilization class for my Africana minor. It started off easy but then intensified to the point that it was driving me crazy.

I had an independent study course with a professor from the Africana department. I knew working with him would be difficult because I had already taken another one of his classes. He worked me all semester, sending me to the library to do hours of research digging through scholarly journals, all so I could come up with a paper. He didn't want me to regurgitate information. He wanted me to think for myself and develop my own opinion about black people and the world.

But it was my last class at Western that challenged me the most that semester. I had made it to page 180 in my third novel. I had the end planned out. I knew where I was going. I had to take one final creative writing class a five thousand–level course. I decided to workshop my book to the class to get help with it from other writers.

I was the only black person in the class. By this time, I was used to that; black people rarely majored in English. The class hated my book. They thought it was racist. They thought I had done nothing but trash white people. It was true that I talked about them a lot. I talked about everyone, including black people. It was during my midterm meeting with the professor from that class that I leaned the most about myself.

"I'm only giving you a B," she told me.

"Why?" I asked.

She looked at me. Her wild, frizzy hair sat atop her head frantically, as if it had a mind of its own mind. "Because you're unable to learn," she said. "You come into class and you put us into a box. You don't listen to us because we're white. You confirmed what I thought about you Wednesday when you made your comment."

In class that Wednesday, we were having a discussion about white people who write from the perspective of black people. We talked about a novelist who had done that, and the white kids thought it was cool. I became angry. I said that I would never read a book like that because a white person could never know what it was truly like to be black. I also said that I wouldn't write from a perspective of a white person because I didn't know what it was like to be white. I guess they thought I was being closed-minded. I was simply telling the truth.

I smiled at her. "You're right," I said. "I wasn't listening to the class because they're white. But I do listen to you. You know what you're talking about. I don't have a problem with white people. I had white friends back in Lansing, but they were different from the kids in the class. I don't know what kind of white people they are."

I decided that I would start being nicer to the class. They were soon to be professionals just like me. They wanted me to listen to them, just as I wanted them to listen to me. It had been only a few months since I finished my fight with the association. I was still learning to trust white people again.

"You're book is all over the place," professor Whitmur told me. "It's a little Terry McMillan, a little drama, a little romance. It feels as if you've taken bits and pieces from other writers and added that into your book. I get the feeling that you've been working on this for a while. I want you to come up with some new work for my class. It's seems like this is your last semester here, and you're gonna do just enough to pass."

I looked at her. "A 'B' is a respectable grade. If all I get is a B, I'll be happy with that. But I will try harder."

She was right about me. I didn't want to write any new material for the semester. I just wanted to edit my book. I had planned to workshop chapter two during the class. I had already begun editing and rewriting. It was almost ready.

Then we moved onto a bigger problem—punctuation and grammar. Half the class did not know how to punctuate dialogue and had major grammatical errors. I was one of them. Professor Whitmur let me know that I would never get published if I didn't learn the rules of English. It didn't matter how great a storyteller I was. Rules were rules.

We talked some more about my writing, and she gave me some great advice.

"Write about what you're thinking about right now. What is on your mind right now?" she asked.

I left my meeting with her in deep thought. I'd been broken down as a writer. Professor Whitmur had opened my eyes to writing. I knew what I wanted to do and be in life. I had an opportunity to do social science writing and write about controversial social events plaguing society, but that wasn't me.

Professor Santos had taught me how to write a great college paper. He taught me how to do scholarly research and write for scholarly journals. But I had already told him that I didn't want to be a revolutionist for a living. Even though I was passionate about black people and our struggle, that's not who I was. I was a creative writer.

Besides, most black people didn't support their leaders. Most black leaders ended up shot in the back of the head, and the black community did nothing about it. Most black leaders didn't make a lot of money, and I wanted to be rich one day. So I decided to focus on my writing.

I left professor Whitmur's office ready to write.

As I sat down at the computer, I thought about the only thing that was on my mind—Green, my condo situation, and Judge Joe Brown. I sat down and wrote my next story for workshop in four weeks.

Next, I had to think of a title. I had taken a poetry class during my spring 2008 semester at WMU. We had talked a lot about titles. The class had hated my titles, and they'd given me great advice for coming up with a title.

"Think about what your poem is about and go with it. Keep it simple," Professor Clay had told me.

I hadn't forgotten his advice. He was one of my role models. I listened to everything Professor Clay had to say.

On the last day of class, he gave his book of poetry away to another student who had won perfect attendance. When I saw his book, I was in shock. So was the rest of the class.

"You're a novelist?" I asked. "Why didn't you tell us?"

"Yeah," another student chimed in. "We've been sitting in class with a novelist all semester, and we didn't even know it," she said.

Professor Clay looked humbled. "It's nothing," he said.

"Getting published is nothing. Just send your work out there. Find publishing companies and send your work to them."

I was inspired just sitting next to him.

I looked at my story, and the title came to me. My story was about my brother Green and Judge Joe Brown, so I called it "Brothers and Judges." Jonathan hated the title, so I came up with "The Expedite."

I work shopped "The Expedite" to the class, and the feedback I got was amazing.

"This is your book," Malcolm, a fellow student told me. "Write this book."

After listening to what the white people had to say, my mind was transformed. I appreciated their opinions and honesty. Never before had I written something so personal. Everything and everyone in the story was real. I'd made nothing up.

"You should think about being a creative nonfiction writer," professor Whitmur told me.

People had told me that my personal life was so crazy that they knew I was gonna write a good book. But I wasn't strong enough to write about myself. I liked hiding behind my characters. I felt protected. Writing about myself made me feel exposed. But I had to do it. I needed to get published.

We talked about the title. I learned that "The Expedite" was grammatically incorrect. I had taken the word from *expedition*, which means to free from hindrance or obstacle. I'd used the word as a noun when, actually, it's a transitive verb. The class, however, loved the title "Brothers and Judges," so I decided to go with that.

One comment in the class caught my attention. Zack, the student who'd received the book as a reward for perfect attendance in poetry, looked at my story and was frustrated. "With a story like this, what's the meaning. Go to China—that's the meaning of this story?"

One of the last scenes featured my discussion with the white man from Kalamazoo at the airport. I gave his comment much thought when I wrote my book. I decided to write a conclusion—or at least try.

I left my workshop on December 3 ready to write my book.

The next day, I shared my experience with Chip. I'd run into him in the Bronco Mall that September and for three months we'd been friends again, although it wasn't the same. He'd had drama with his wife, and that's why he hadn't been around. Once he came back into my life, it was time for me to go.

Chip had previously read the first chapter of *Soul Mourning* and loved it. "Don't let the white people change you," he said. "You're raw and edgy. Never lose that. White people will fuck with you, but they'll try to calm you down first. I like the title *The Expedite*. It's different. Don't do everything the white people say."

I nodded my head in agreement. He was right. To be a writer is to deal with the changes that people will try to bestow upon me. I realized then that I had to be prepared and know who I was before I got out there.

I promised to write *Brothers and Judges* as soon as I graduated. I even told my teacher that I would send it to her as soon as it was done. My plan was to finish out the semester, move to Nashville, and start work on my new book. I pushed *Soul Mourning* to the back of my list. I felt *Brothers and Judges* had a better chance of making it. After all, who doesn't want to read about cool celebrities and family drama?

All I had to do next was make it to graduation day. I decided that, if by some chance I failed a class, I would still leave for Nashville. I would figure out a way to make the class up later. It was time to leave Kalamazoo. I'd learned all there was to learn there. I was twenty-seven years old. I'd grown up at Western. My experience there had made me the person I was now.

I knew no one in my family would be there for my graduation ceremony. I had told the class that on Wednesday night, two days before the ceremony. "I know they're gonna do something," I said. "Either they're going be late, or they won't be able to make it. I know my family. They won't be there. I don't care, though. This is my moment, and I'm not letting anyone take that from me."

"Well I'll be there," Professor Whitmur said to me. "You know that you have at least one friend there."

I was right. Mom called me two days before the ceremony and told me that Yellow wasn't coming. She didn't know why; Yellow hadn't said why she couldn't make it. I called Yellow and left her a message. She called me back Friday, but I didn't get the call. I called her back twice, but she never called me back.

Yellow was supposed to drive Mom down. Then Jonathan was to have returned with them to Lansing. My friend, Jonah, was coming that Friday to pack up the U-Haul, and I was leaving Kalamazoo right after graduation. The ceremony was set for 9:00 a.m. I wanted to be on the road by 2:00 that afternoon.

Since Yellow wasn't coming, Mom had no ride. I had to take Jonathan to Lansing early, so he wouldn't be at the ceremony. Perhaps I could have waited to go to Lansing, but there was little time. Jonah had to be back to work that Monday. I didn't want to wait for the GM holiday shutdown in ten days to leave Kalamazoo. I wanted to spend Christmas in Nashville.

"Don't worry," I told Jonathan. "I'ma order the graduation DVD. We can watch it together. You've already seen me graduate from college once. It's no big deal."

He understood. I took him to Lansing that Friday night. I dropped him off at Mom's and took Jonah to drop his car off at his sister's house. We then headed back to Kalamazoo to start loading the truck.

Dad called me that night. Once again, he wanted to know how I'd made it. "Me and your grandma was sitting here talking trying to figure out how you graduated. I said that it's that boy that keeps you motivated."

This time I had an answer for him. Unlike during the conversation following my LCC graduation, I understood myself. "Honestly, Dad," I replied. "I was always a good student. I was always in the band and on the honor roll. I would have graduated whether or not I had a baby."

Dad had nothing more to say. He let out a simple "Oh," and ended our conversation.

I hung up the phone, proud that I had let him know what a great child I'd always been. Yes, I started having sex at thirteen. Yes, I had a baby at sixteen. Yes, I skipped a lot of school and talked back to my teachers. I cursed and got into fights, but I never stopped being a good kid or a good student—never.

I found out that my dad wasn't coming to my graduation ceremony either because he had to work. I didn't mind. Like I said before, it was my moment. I wasn't letting anyone take that away from me.

I had over forty-five boxes packed, but there was still more to go. Plus, I had to clean. We worked all night until we were tired. Chip came by to help, but he did little more than watch. I think it was because he was upset that he couldn't take me to Nashville. Chip's friend had backed out and Jonah's friend showed up.

Plus Jonah didn't want Chip there. "Me and my boy, we got it," Jonah told me when I suggested Chip's help.

Men don't mix, and so I understood how Jonah felt.

I awoke graduation morning excited. I wasn't upset that no one in my family would be at the ceremony. I had spent the entire two and a half years at WMU alone. Even though my son was there, he was my child and not my friend. College was a path that I walked by myself. In my mind, it was God's will—my destiny—that no one was there with me. I had to make that final walk by myself.

It didn't hit me that I was there alone until I heard my name being called. No applause followed. The auditorium was silent as I cat-walked onto stage. I didn't care. I smiled, did my walk, shook hands with the dean, and was excited to be graduating from college. I saw professor Whitmur on stage with the other faculty, and I knew I wasn't completely alone.

Chip was late, so he missed my name being called. I wasn't

upset. He bought me a card and some roses for graduation, and we went out on campus and took pictures with me in my cap and gown.

Chip and I laughed at the fact that I tripped up the stairs once again. I didn't see him until I stood back up. "Did you see me fall?" I asked him trying to remain cool.

"Yeah I did. You wouldn't be Nova if you wasn't trippin' and falling."

I smiled. So caught up in my own mind, I was always tripping over my feet, which are already big for a girl. I tripped on my stairs at Whitehall almost every day. I told myself that, after I left Kalamazoo, I would start paying more attention to my feet, even if I did wear a size nine.

We didn't get done packing and cleaning until nearly four that morning. Jonah his friend, Brian, and I headed out for Nashville at seven in the morning. The leasing office through which I was leasing my new apartment was open until four. If we didn't make it by then, I wouldn't be able to move in until Monday. It would be tight. I had to sign my lease, unload the truck, turn around, and go back to Lansing to drop Jonah and Brian off. Then I'd head to Kalamazoo to wrap up my last bit of business, and finally, I'd head back to Lansing to say good-bye to Mom and pick up Jonathan.

All of that was on my mind as I merged on to 69 South. It wasn't time to say my final good-bye to Michigan; I would do that once I came back north.

* * *

I arrived back in Kalamazoo late Sunday evening. I spent the night with Vernon and got dressed at his house. On Monday, I turned in the keys to my apartment and my cable box. I spent the day hanging with Chip. Before I left Kalamazoo for good, I had one final good-bye.

I stopped by Raheem's apartment before I left for Lansing to pick up Jonathan and return to Nashville. Raheem and I sat in my car talking face-to-face for the last time.

"I can't believe it's over. It went so fast. I think about everything I went through here. I went through some real shit here, but it was worth it. I got my degree," I said. I turned and faced Raheem. "You were my first friend here. You were the first person I met."

Raheem looked at me. "And I'm the last person you're saying good-bye to."

I turned away and wiped a tear from my eyes. I loved Raheem. He was one of the realest people I'd ever met. We'd had our ups and downs, but our friendship was real. I ended up going into Raheem's apartment to lie down for a few hours before hitting the highway. Raheem had to leave, and so I stayed in his room and slept. He woke me up some time around twelve. He had plans with his girlfriend, so I couldn't spend the night. I understood.

Raheem and I hugged one last time. "Don't be an asshole," he told me as I walked out the door.

I laughed. "I won't. I'll call you when I get to Nashville."

Chapter Eighteen:
Epilogue

College is over, at least for now. My relationship with Green is different. I no longer trust him and feel nervous when he's around. I stopped with the random phone threats months ago, I'd begun making threatening phone calls to him sometime in late January 2008 and I stopped with my telephone death threats that May. I now let him have peace in his new life.

Green moved out of our mom's house and into his own apartment in September 2008. He now takes care of his son and enjoys being a father. He's still looking for work as a telemarketer.

I gave the condo back to GMAC. GMAC called me harassing me about a late payment, and I had had enough. I told them that I was disabled and couldn't afford the payments. I asked what I could do.

After hearing my options, I made my decision. I stopped paying the mortgage and began the process of signing all interests in the condo over to the company by a deed in *Lieu of foreclosure*, a program designed to help people who cannot afford their mortgage payment due to circumstances beyond their control.

Ironically, if I'd given the house back to GMAC as soon as I moved to Kalamazoo, I wouldn't have had to rent my condo out and lose $16,000 in association charges (they kept adding charges to my account and so by the time I left Kalamazoo the final bill was over $16,000), pay $7,000 worth of mortgage payments to GMAC while the condo sat empty, sue my little brother on national television, or spend my whole college experience stressed about my life in Lansing.

But that was how life was. Hindsight was twenty-twenty, and a learning lesson was nothing more than a mind fuck.

Yet, no words can express the pain of losing my condo. I was no longer a homeowner. I had deferred my dream. Or, perhaps it had evaporated. I had it all, and I lost it.

And no I'm not happy with the way things turned out. I feel as if I had been used and then discarded by all those around me. I hope that my brother and the condo association pay for what they have done to me and my life. It wasn't fair the way I was mistreated and since moving to Nashville I have been slapped in the face by reality. Green, I no longer hate you but, I hope you rot in hell!

Being back on the bottom has been humbling and insightful. I feel as if I'm back on the West side of Lansing, scrounging around the hood, barefoot and definitely broke. But I know God is still with me, and that keeps me going.

The hurt I feel cannot be hidden by the passage of days. Anxiety strikes me whenever I think about repaying the association. I've gotten over my hatred and anger toward white people, although sometimes it resurfaces when I think about the association. Then I think about the MDCR, and it subsides.

I've been poverty-poor since moving to Nashville. I have no money left and no one to ask for help. I stay one step ahead of the eviction notices, shutoffs, and disconnections. Every day, I pray that my life changes.

I've lost some of the twenty-five pounds I gained in college. It's a struggle to keep the weight off while I go through my depression, but I manage.

I still have my job at GM. I decided not to take a buyout or try to sue them. I want to ride GM out to the end. No matter what, I plan on staying with GM, if for no other reason than sentimental value. I hope one day GM can recover.

I will never forget Western Michigan University, the people I met there, or the experiences I had. College was great; it was hard, trying, and character building. I'm thankful I was able to go. Most single, African American, teenage mothers never make it out of the hood. I made it all the way through college.

I passed all my classes my last semester and graduated with an overall grade point average of 3.0—meeting the goal I'd originally set for myself. It was hard, but I did it. I've proven to myself that I'm smart, if only book smart.

I've stopped crying. I've realized that life is a process; one action precedes another, and so I pace along, ignoring the "Due Immediately" notices the association sends to my door.

As a substitute teacher in Nashville, I've seen many things. I've witnessed hurt and pain on so many levels from so many children. But one particular school—Bailey Middle School—showed me the most.

Never before had I witnessed such poverty and desolation; and never before had I witnessed as much hope. The African American community always has been and always will be a symbol of strength and pride in the world. Bailey showed me the true inner-city struggle. And so I'll close with this poem, which I give to the children of Bailey Middle School and all the inner-city kids of the world.

A Prayer Poem
(I dedicate this poem to the eighties babies and beyond!)[1]

Terror strikes in the late night.
Fearful children lay splattered, shivering,
quivering, battered. I hear kicks and slaps,
Screams and then collapse!
Brown bodies, blue bruises, black man
Who always abuses … his gifts, yet he feels he's cursed
And what's worse? Watch their worth
Disintegrate with time.
LISTEN TO THE CHURCH BELLS CHIME.
SILENT. AMONG THE DEATH EARS WHO FEARS
No one but man, strong with his fists, who lift
Their spirits then leaves them broken,
Crumpled on the floor to rise no more
And be who they are.
Stars fallen from Heaven
Everyman's blessin'.
The adolescent runs free, aimlessly in search of church but
It cannot be found. SO let it resound. The pain
And the sorrow until tomorrow or a better day. Now
Let us pray.
God forgive us for all our sins until the end
Time slowly ticktocking; he'll be watching
Who? God and the Devil … Amen.

---

1   No other generation has experienced the horror of living in the modern
    world like the children of the nineteen eighties and beyond. And in my
    opinion this is the case all around the world. We have been taken advantage
    of by the previous generations to the point that there is nothing left. I hope
    that my readers will take this poem as an inspiration to our struggle. It is
    too late for change and we all know it. Change should have come decades
    ago. Now all we can do is pray and wait for the return of GOD.

Manufactured By: RR Donnelley
                     Breinigsville, PA USA
                     February, 2011